ESKY

Esky

The Early Years at <u>Esquire</u>

HUGH MERRILL

Rutgers University Press

New Brunswick, New Jersey

Illustrations from *Esquire* are reproduced by permission of The Hearst
Corporation. All rights reserved.

Library of Congress Cataloging-in-Publication Data

Merrill, Hugh.
    Esky : the early years at Esquire / Hugh Merrill.
        p.   cm.
    Includes bibliographical references and index.
    ISBN 0-8135-2165-3
    1. Esquire (New York : N.Y.)   I. Title.
PN4900.E8M47 1995   94-39575
051—dc20   CIP

British Cataloging-in-Publication information available

Copyright © 1995 by Hugh Merrill
All rights reserved
Published by Rutgers University Press, New Brunswick, N.J.
Manufactured in the United States of America

For Jacinta
and for The Queen of the Blues

In memory of
Mary Sherrill

Contents

Acknowledgments

Many people have given freely of their time and energy to make *Esky* a reality.

I want to thank Reid Austin, Frances Birmingham, Abe Blinder, Jeanne Dean, Oscar Dystel, Jerry Jontry, and Martin Mayer for taking time to be interviewed about their memories of the early days at *Esquire*. Without their help, the characters and events in the book would not be as complete.

For the writer of nonfiction, a reference librarian is like an angel of mercy. Three have been especially helpful to me—Karen L. Jania at the Bentley Historical Library at the University of Michigan, Theresa Johnson at the John C. Pace Library at the University of West Florida, and Marie Nitchkie at the Robert W. Woodruff Library at Emory University. Without their help I might still be mired in stacks of papers and books. Also helpful were the staff members of Page and Palette Books in Pensacola—Donna Anderson, Candace Bennett, and Jovanna Stanley. They helped me find obscure volumes quickly and ignored my grousing.

At Emory University, I am grateful to David Cook, Christine Levenduski, and Allen Tullos, who all helped me with expert advice and steered me in the right direction when I was confused and bewildered.

I am also grateful to Beverly Couch, who helped me prepare the manuscript; to my agent, Jane Dystel of Jane Dystel Literary Management; and to Leslie Mitchner, my editor at Rutgers University Press.

For moral support I want to thank Ernie and Donna Elligson, Julie Hairston, Rosemary Little, Pat Murdock, Jim and Carol O'Kon, and David Parrish. They are good friends who, I suspect, feigned interest in *Esquire* when any of a thousand topics would have been more interesting.

Finally, I want to thank my wife, Jacinta, who encouraged this project and stood by me the whole way. Without her love and support, it never would have been possible.

ESKY

Introduction

If the United States were really the land depicted in supermarket tabloids, there would be a headline screaming from the racks at checkout counters announcing that Tina Brown, the editor of *The New Yorker*, was the secret, illegitimate daughter of Arnold Gingrich, the founding editor of *Esquire*.

That is not true, of course, but Brown's editing style and her ability to grab headlines with the magazines she edits—first *Vanity Fair* and now *The New Yorker*—match what Gingrich did when *Esquire* first hit the newsstands in 1933. In 1938, a critic named Henry Pringle accused Gingrich of forming an "unholy combination of erudition and sex" and compared the contents of the magazine to having Thomas Mann or Ernest Hemingway or John Dos Passos read aloud from his works at a burlesque show. *Esquire* has always been heavy on literature—Ernest Hemingway, F. Scott Fitzgerald, Dashiell Hammett, and Erskine Caldwell have been among the magazine's contributors—but it has also been the home of the risqué cartoons of E. Simms Campbell and the "girlie" art of Vargas and Petty. *Esquire* celebrated jazz when no other magazine did, and it always emphasized fashion and correctness. It was flashy, and it was literary. It was bawdy, yet it emphasized the style of the upper classes.

Fifty-five years after Pringle wrote about *Esquire*'s unholy alliance for *Scribner's*, a profile of Tina Brown in the *New York Times Magazine* accused *The New Yorker* editor of packaging titillation for sophisticated tastes. What Gingrich did in the 1930s and 1940s, and what Brown is doing today, is to mix the brassy world of pop culture with the genteel domain of high culture. And, like *Esquire* in the 1930s, that mixture at the once staid and proper *New Yorker* sets tongues fluttering and eyes popping. What was Thomas Mann doing in a magazine that featured the pinup paintings of George Petty and Alberto Vargas? What are nude photographs of an actress and paintings by comic-book artists doing in a magazine that deified John Updike and Rachael Carson?

In both cases, this mixture of pop and high culture is selling magazines and advertising. In its first issue, in the midst of the Great Depression, *Esquire* sold 100,000 copies at fifty cents each, and within a few years it had a circulation of 700,000. Since Tina Brown took over as editor of *The New Yorker*, circulation has increased 20 percent and advertising has risen by 14 percent. Of course, the pace of change in the magazine industry today has greatly accelerated from the 1930s when *Esquire* started. Specialization has fragmented the reading audience, and more and more titles compete for the same audience. But Brown, like Gingrich, is looking for a mass market with appeal to various audiences within one magazine.

Magazine historian Theodore Peterson said Gingrich's editing style combined a heavy load of excellence with a fine streak of vulgarity. Martin Mayer, who worked with Gingrich as a copy editor at *Esquire*, remembers Gingrich saying that a magazine is like a three-ring circus. If you go to a circus and find you like every one of the acts, Mayer explains, that's a lousy circus. It's the recollection of two or three acts that brings you back next year, and different people go for different acts. Certainly this is the same philosophy Tina Brown has adopted. In *The New York Times* she is quoted as talking about a "mixed pace" for her magazine; at *Vanity Fair* she mixed stories on Gorbachev and Goldie Hawn; even a story about a world leader often contained the thrill of sex and violence. Her circus is filled with different acts just as Gingrich's was.

The *New York Times Magazine* said the Brown formula "would include long, 10,000-word articles like those found in more intellectual journals, but also indulge in the kind of star-struck celebrity profiles found on supermarket checkout lines. It would create a new niche that it alone could occupy; it would be smarter than anything glossier and glossier than anything smarter."

Brown has gotten so much publicity because her concept of a magazine seems so new and outrageous, and because she has taken a bastion of high culture and invited the masses into the tent. Most of her publicity credits her with a new kind of magazine, but that's because few journalists bother with history. If they did, they would know that this unholy alliance of high and low culture first astounded

Americans in 1933 in the pages of *Esquire*. This book is about how that mixture first showed up in American journalism, and about how two men from Chicago whose main ambition was to sell advertising for men's clothes created a new genre, the respectable men's magazine. It is also about how that magazine and its corporate symbol, Esky, the popeyed man-about-town who appeared on every *Esquire* cover, paved the way for magazines like *Playboy*, *The Evergreen Review*, and Tina Brown's *New Yorker*. It is a story about merchandising, censorship, sex, literature, ideas, bawdy humor, and fashion.

This is more than a book about one magazine from decades ago. The story of *Esquire*'s early days is, in many ways, a blueprint for the most outrageous and successful consumer magazines of the 1990s.

The show's about to begin, and the tent is almost full. In ring one . . . Hefner! The Incredible Hefner and his hutch of trained bunnies! In ring three . . . the charming, ever-lovely, and delightful . . . Tina! The Magnificent Tina Brown, America's greatest quick-change artist! And in the center ring . . . Esky! The irrepressible ringmaster who brought together for the first time on this or any continent a magical mixture of ladies, literature, and lampoons sure to delight sophisticated audiences everywhere! Esky!

Hurry! Hurry! Hurry!

When a Highbrow
Meets a Lowbrow

hen *Esquire* magazine was first published in the fall of 1933, Arnold Gingrich, its editor and unofficial publicist, announced that his creation was the first American magazine for men. Maybe it was the first U.S. magazine to *call* itself that, but magazines for men go back to the beginning of this country's publications. There were obvious early examples like *Burton's Gentleman's Magazine* (1830), edited by William E. Burton, a famous actor of the time, but the idea of a magazine edited and published primarily for a male audience is far wider than the titles of publications would lead you to believe.

For all of the nineteenth century, and much of the twentieth, most magazines, unless otherwise specified (*Godey's Lady's Book* and *The Ladies' Home Journal*, for example), were primarily for a male audience, even though they occasionally carried features for women. Even a magazine like *The Saturday Evening Post*, which became a publication for the entire family, was initially a businessman's journal. *Esquire*'s difference was in exploiting the market for advertising directed toward male consumers, a field that no magazine had tried before.

American magazines first gained a foothold in the mass market in the 1890s. Several factors contributed to this development. The expansion of the railroads after the Civil War created a national market for goods that could be moved swiftly from factory to retailer. The postal act of March 3, 1879, guaranteed low mailing rates for magazines, and the development of the rotary press by R. Hoe and Company in 1886 plus the invention of the rotary web press by C. B. Cottrell and Sons Company added speed to the printing process. The new printing presses also used halftone reproductions of photographs, which meant illustration was no longer limited to expensive engravings or sketches. Then, in 1908, Cottrell installed the first multicolor rotary press for the Curtis Publishing Company. With color and photographs, magazines were to Americans of the early twentieth century what television would be five decades later—a factory manufacturing wishes and desires.

It was the explosion of advertising, not legal or technical innovation, that made mass magazine publishing profitable. There were, of course, profitable magazines that relied only on subscription revenue, but they were not aimed at the large audiences that publishing giants like Curtis were pursuing. Magazines like *The Reader's Digest*, first published in 1922, made healthy profits without advertising, but they were the exception. Of course, American magazines had carried advertising since colonial times, but it was usually placed in the back pages and read like today's classifieds. Then, in 1870, *Scribner's* (1870–1939) and *Harper's* (founded in 1850) started offering low rates to advertisers who bought full pages. Another publisher, Cyrus H. K. Curtis, founded the *Ladies' Home Journal* in 1883 with subscription prices at fifty cents per year. That was one-sixth the price of *Godey's Lady's Book,* which, until then, had been the leading American women's magazine. Godey's top circulation was 150,000, but it declined after the Civil War and died in 1883.[1]

By 1900 Curtis had a million subscribers and had established the formula for magazines that served the market by entertaining the masses: low newsstand and subscription costs and high revenue from advertising. The same strategy of low costs for the reader and high profits from advertising spread from women's magazines into the general circulation field when Frank Munsey lowered the price of *Munsey's Magazine* from a quarter to a dime in 1883, when S. S. McClure dropped the newsstand price of *McClure's* from fifteen cents to a dime the following year, and when Curtis brought out the *Saturday Evening Post* in 1890. It was a formula that would remain unchanged for the next forty years.

All of these magazines were for that part of the masses that would be most profitable to advertisers—the white, middle-class, business-oriented reader. Magazines that Gingrich considered to be *Esquire's* competitors, however—*Town and Country* (founded in 1846), *American Mercury* (founded in 1924), and *Vanity Fair* (founded in 1913)—

catered to a smaller segment of the population. For *Town and Country* it was "the upper ten thousand composed of the well-born, the rich and the able."[2] The *American Mercury* celebrated iconoclasm and debunked the mores of middle-class American life, and *Vanity Fair* emphasized topics discussed at upper-crust cocktail parties—painting, tapestries, rare books, smart dresses, dances, gardens, country houses, correct cuisine, and pretty women.[3] At first glance, it seems odd that *Esquire*, a magazine best known in its first two decades for raunchy humor and girlie pictures, would consider itself a competitor to publications for the nation's educated elite, and yet Gingrich was more right about his magazine than public opinion at the time was.

Judging from the first press accounts of *Esquire*, the magazine was perceived as a fancier version of *Captain Billy's Whiz Bang*, a post–World War I magazine of off-color jokes published by Wilford H. Fawcett; *Smokehouse Monthly*, a similar magazine also published by Fawcett; the *Calgary Eye-Opener*, published by Fawcett's wife, Antoinette Fisher Fawcett, after they were divorced; and *Ballyhoo*, published in the early 1930s by Dell. All of them were best known for jokes about sex and bodily functions, and none of them pretended to have a particular appeal to the upper crust. They were magazines of mass, not class.

More charitable readers might have seen similarities between *Esquire* and *Judge* (1881–1937) or the pre-Luce *Life* (1883–1936). Both were sophisticated humor magazines that emphasized wit and charm. *Judge* was first published in 1881 and lasted until 1936, when the Depression and competition from *The New Yorker* (founded in 1925) became too much for it. *Life*, begun two years later than *Judge*, was a creation of a former Harvard *Lampoon* editor. In addition to its humor, *Life* was the home of the Gibson Girl, the figure made famous in drawings by Charles Dana Gibson that established beauty standards for American women in the first two decades of the century, and the flapper drawings of John Held, Jr., which did the same for the young women of the Roaring Twenties.

Neither *Judge* nor *Life* was as frankly sexual as *Esquire*, a magazine with pinups, scores of full-color cartoons, and fiction by reputable authors. It was the sexuality that gave the magazine its notoriety as men throughout the country reached into their pockets for money to buy the high-priced (fifty-cent) magazine. At first glance, the cartoons and girlie pictures seemed reminiscent of burlesque, but that's not quite accurate. Burlesque was a theatrical form with no snob appeal, and snob appeal was part of what *Esquire* wanted. Like *Esquire*, burlesque featured sexual humor and seminude women, but the baldheaded men in the front-row seats were not bankers and investors. Burlesque was remarkably democratic. And it may have been this democracy that got it into trouble. Whatever its charm may have been, burlesque lacked respectability, and that led to censorship. Burlesque was a nineteenth-century form grounded in the aesthetics of transgression, inversion, and the grotesque. It was a sort of low other that was outside the social order but, at the same time, the object of desire or fascination.[4] It was as an object of desire that burlesque got into trouble in the twentieth century. In 1908, Millie de Leon, the Odalisque of the East, was occasionally arrested in New York for appearing without tights; three years earlier Olga Nethersole was arrested in the same city after she permitted herself to be kissed on the mouth and dragged to a theatrical bedroom. The censorship continued through the 1930s when police raided the Eltinge Theater in New York because the comics' dialogue had double meanings.[5] Burlesque, theatrical eroticism for the masses, was always in trouble. But it was a different story when burlesque went uptown and was made over into the *Ziegfeld Follies*.

Florenz Ziegfeld (1867–1932) was an American showman with the remarkable ability to transform popular, lowbrow entertainment into theatrical productions for the wealthy and high-born. In 1893 he promoted a circus strongman, The Great Sandow, at the Trocadero Theater in Chicago. Ziegfeld had special music composed to be played while Sandow held a man in the palm of his hand, opened a safe with his teeth, bent a poker, and balanced weights up to three hundred pounds. After Sandow's performance, Ziegfeld walked on stage and announced that any woman willing to contribute three hundred dollars to charity could come backstage and feel the strongman's biceps. Mrs. Potter Palmer, the wife of the hotel magnate, and Mrs. George Pullman, the wife of the industrialist who made railroad cars, stood up, made their contribution, then walked backstage to cop their three-hundred-dollar feel.[6] The sideshow was now above the salt. The Midas touch of the wives of millionaires had made carny trash respectable.

What Ziegfeld did for a sideshow novelty act, he later did for burlesque. From 1907 through 1931 the *Ziegfeld Follies* presented more than three thousand chorus girls in various stages of undress to New York audiences who paid five dollars a ticket to see them. Across town, burlesque offered a similar show for seventy-five cents. There was a difference, of course. Ziegfeld's show added music by composers like Irving Berlin, breathtaking costumes, and lavish stage sets. Ziegfeld promoted himself as the Glorifier of the American Girl, and the marquee where the *Follies* played proclaimed, "Through these doors walk the most beautiful girls in the world." And, unlike burlesque, none of the Ziegfeld Girls was ever arrested for indecent exposure. That's not surprising. A look at the history of pornography shows that in Victorian times frankly sexual material was available in museums with limited access, in medical and technical literature, and in the classical education of gentlemen.[7] What was available for the aristocrat and the educated was kept out of sight from everyone else for fear it would corrupt them. This was no more apparent anywhere than in the contrast of public attitudes on burlesque and the *Ziegfeld Follies*. Nudity in a legitimate theater for five dollars a ticket was permissible, but when a woman stripped on stage at a grind house on Forty-second Street where tickets cost seventy-five cents, she was likely to be hustled off to jail. *Esquire*, then, aspired to be the *Ziegfeld Follies* of magazine publishing, leaving the mass burlesque audience to publications like *Ballyhoo* and *Smokehouse Monthly*.

In fact, despite the increasing popularity of the movies, it was Broadway and the impact of Ziegfeld and similar shows (*The Greenwich Village Follies, Earl Carroll's Vanities, George White's Scandals*) that most influenced *Esquire*. Hollywood may have been moving into the public consciousness in the 1930s, but that decade was one that also felt the enormous influence of the Great White Way. Some of the new industrial designers who were busy redesigning America came from the theater. Norman Bel Geddes, who helped to popularize streamlining, was a set designer on Broadway; so was Henry Dryfuss, who redesigned products with what he called "cleanlining."[8] A decade later, Hollywood would have a monopoly on popular taste, but in the years that shaped *Esquire*, America still whistled a Broadway melody. Of course, by the time *Esquire* was first published, Broadway had been incorporated into Hollywood through vehicles like the Busby Berkeley musicals. Although there were both stars and chorus girls in both Hollywood and Broadway, it was the idea of Broadway and stage performers that shaped *Esquire.*

For example, there are the famous "girl" paintings (most notably by George Petty and Albert Vargas) that were the magazine's most popular feature. None of the women in the paintings had names; they were just that month's model. They were like chorus girls—beautiful, anonymous, presented for a passing or lingering glance in an unreal setting. In the movies, however, the star system that began in the 1910s gave names and personalities to beautiful women. They were real, concrete. Fan magazines described their private lives, their families. There was little anonymity in Hollywood, but on Broadway and in *Esquire* a pretty girl was, indeed, like a melody—ethereal and fleeting, with no substance. Chorus girls existed only on stage; once the show was over they were just pretty women without the feathers and makeup that had transformed them. *Esquire*'s "girls" were equally unreal: they existed only on paper, to be forgotten when the new model appeared a month later.

There were other similarities between the world of Broadway and *Esquire.* The magazine's cartoons often showed beautiful women, glittering with jewelry, in the company of old, substantial gentlemen. Compare that with a description of a Ziegfeld Girl in *The Ziegfeld Follies* by Marjorie Farnsworth:

> To be labeled a Ziegfeld Girl was the dream of innumerable maidens and otherwise throughout all of America, and a goodly portion of the world. Their average salary was $75 a week but they wore ermines, sables, mink and diamonds. And if anyone gave a party for them—and some astonishing people did—they took for granted emeralds or at least thousand dollar bills tucked into vanity cases as their just due.[9]

Or, as a woman in her underwear examining jewelry says to a stout old man in a dinner jacket in an *Esquire* cartoon, "Of course, our friendship is all that matters."

As audiences dwindled and more people turned their attention to the movies, Florenz Ziegfeld *Follies* closed in 1931, two years before *Esquire* was first published. But David Smart, *Esquire*'s publisher, worked to keep the Ziegfeld spirit alive. He hired a Ziegfeld poster artist, Alberto Vargas, to draw the *Esquire* "girls"; he married Edna Gabrielle Richards who, under the name Gaby Dure, had been a Ziegfeld girl. On a photograph of himself that he gave to Vargas, Smart wrote, "To my talented friends Al Vargas and his good wife Anna Mae who labor like slaves to perpetuate the Ziegfeld tradition so that *Esquire* can boast 'Through these pages walk (and lie) the most beautiful girls in the world.'"[10]

It's no wonder, then, that two years after *Esquire*'s first issue Richard Rodgers and Lorenz Hart proposed bringing back shows like the *Ziegfeld Follies* by staging *Esquire Girls of 1935*. The show was never mounted, however, because neither David Smart nor his brother Alfred had ever heard of Rodgers and Hart.[11]

Ziegfeld, writes Marjorie Farnsworth, "knew the subtle line between desire and lust, between good taste and vulgarity, and never crossed it."[12] Years later, magazine historian Theodore Peterson would write about *Esquire* editor Arnold Gingrich, "I could spot any magazine he edited because each bore his trademark—a heavy load of excellence with a fine streak of vulgarity."[13] It sounds almost as if they were writing about the same man.

There was another reason that *Esquire* paid more attention to the stage than to the screen, and that was censorship. The problems of Millie De Leon and Olga Nethersole were nothing compared to what motion pictures had endured. As early as 1909 there was state and local censorship of movies, and in 1915 the U.S. Supreme Court ruled that the First Amendment did not apply to film. Add to that the industry-imposed censorship of the Motion Picture Producers and Distributors of America, Inc., which began in 1917, and it's apparent that movies were not the medium that would inspire a daring new magazine for men, even though the stricter censorship code was not established until the early 1930s. Until then, Hollywood got away with a lot, including nudity and overt sexuality. And, out of the mainstream, there were more explicit films than the studios would allow. For one hundred to two hundred dollars a reel (the equivalent of one thousand to two thousand dollars today), rich men could buy hard-core "cooch reels." There were also a few exploitation producers showing soft-core sex films around the country, but these were considered somewhat low-class, not the stuff *Esquire* would be interested in.[14] Even though censorship made Hollywood's films seem tame by today's standards, the story line of some films showed that there would be plenty of interest in what the new "Magazine for Men" would offer. During the 1920s, 419 films produced by the major studios dealt with flappers, actresses, and models. That was 8.44 percent of all films released during that decade.[15] These films, like *Esquire*, often had Broadway at their core.

This framework of Ziegfeldian sex and comedy was not what shocked critics most about *Esquire* when it appeared in 1933. Rather, it was the mixture of those elements, which were considered low or popular culture, with literature by critically acclaimed authors, which was considered high culture. Writing in *Scribner's*, a high-culture magazine of the thirties, Henry Pringle compared *Esquire* to having Thomas Mann or Ernest Hemingway read aloud from their works at a burlesque show. He called it an "unholy combination."[16] *Time* called *Esquire* a "*Scribner's* to the Smoking Room."[17]

It is not surprising that this mixture of high and low culture could outrage critics. In the late 1880s, America began what Lawrence W. Levine calls "the sacralization of culture." Until that time Shakespeare, Italian opera, and art museums were as much the property of the working class as the brahmins. That began to change as the twentieth century approached. In the 1890s, the prevailing romantic tradition said the artist's vocation should be a "religion." In 1892 the critic Henry C. Finck wrote that popular music occupied a lesser region than symphonic music.[18] Nowhere was this separation of culture into realms of the high and the low more apparent than in the 1893 Columbian Exposition in Chicago. For the educated, there was the White City, the Court of Honor with marbled buildings of classical architecture. For the masses, just outside the gate, was the midway, with a Ferris wheel and Little Egypt doing a hoochie-coochie dance. The midway was purposely separated from White City, according to the president of the exposition's board of directors, to prevent "jarring contrasts" between "the beautiful buildings and grounds and the illimitable exhibits" of White City and the "amusing, distracting, ludicrous, and noisy attractions" of the midway.[19] In other words, culture was serious business for the educated. Fun, on the other hand, was frivolity for the masses. It would be improper for the two to mix. They should be separated by a barrier as real as the unseen wall between social classes.

And it was this barrier that *Esquire* stormed and broke down. Gingrich wanted an audience interested in high culture because his advertisers—primarily manufacturers of expensive menswear—needed to appeal to someone with enough income to buy new clothes and consider fashion important. At the same time, he wanted a manly emphasis. That was provided by sex. The sex and the literature were actually camouflage for the magazine's real purpose—selling advertising. And, although Gingrich didn't know it, this mixture of high and low cultures helped create an opening in the wall of American cultural separation. *Esquire* could give an uneducated man curvaceous cuties to ogle and expose him to Hemingway on the next page. The magazine could take the erudite reader of Thomas Mann and give him a quick hubba-hubba thrill with his shot of culture. It was as if Little Egypt had been moved from the midway to White City; as if the Ferris wheel and the marbled buildings of the Court of Honor were granted equality. *Esquire* was one of several cultural productions that strained the barriers of cultural separation during the next two decades. Another was Hollywood, whose studios had both high culture (MGM) and mass culture (Warner Brothers). By the 1960s, the wall between high and low had collapsed, and that change was ushered in by *Esquire* as well as by the movie studios. Being part of the beginning of that change in American culture is quite an accomplishment for two men who really only wanted to sell readers a new shirt and tie.

2   Gingrich and Smart: The Days before *Esquire*

agazine historian Theodore Peterson, who considers Arnold Gingrich one of the twentieth century's great magazine editors, said his secret was a mixture of excellence with a streak of vulgarity. As examples he cited the scantily clad pinups followed with fiction by Thomas Mann in the early issues of *Esquire*.[1] That mixture of vulgarity with excellence has roots in Gingrich's working-class background and his struggle to become a sophisticate. Although he was able to go beyond his origins in his appreciation for "literature" and "art," he remained in touch with the tastes of the majority of the country's nonsophisticates. Unlike a member of the elite, he was always an amateur in high culture, teaching himself the violin, forging his own literary interests without much instruction. He spoke in gruff, homely similes, reducing even the most complicated idea in a way businessmen could understand.

Both Peterson and Martin Mayer, who was a copy editor for *Esquire* under Gingrich, talk about Gingrich's wide range of interests, his never-ending curiosity. A real sophisticate would be less likely to be in touch with subjects beyond the narrow range of genteel topics in vogue in cafe society. A self-made sophisticate could cheerfully mix a short story by F. Scott Fitzgerald with the frankly sexual burlesque cartoons of E. Simms Campbell without giving a thought to incongruity. Gingrich's *Esquire* was a unique mixture of the high culture of literature and the low culture of bawdy jokes. Gingrich's background—he was the son of a Michigan woodcarver and a sophisticate who loved Mozart and Hemingway—gave him his editing style.

Arnold Gingrich was born in Grand Rapids, Michigan, on December 5, 1903. His father, John Gingrich, was descended from Michael Gingrich, who immigrated to the United States from the countryside around Basel, Switzerland, about 1747. The early American Gingriches were followers of Menno Simon, the founder of the Mennonite religion, and settled in what is now Lebanon County, Pennsylvania. "The original family was divided," wrote Arnold Gingrich, "as a result of a doctrinal dispute, sometime between 1775 and 1800 and all those members of the congregation who believed a certain way stayed put, while all the dissidents packed up Conestoga wagons and moved bag and baggage (with bags of silver coins under the wagon seats) to the sandhills of Waterloo County, Ontario."[2]

The first Canadian Gingriches were farmers, but John Gingrich, Arnold's grandfather, moved to Berlin, Ontario, and became a blacksmith. He lived in several Ontario towns, moving frequently from Floradale to Preston to Berlin. He remained a Mennonite. His son, Arnold's father, John Hembling Gingrich, was born in 1876 and learned woodcarving, which would become his profession. He stayed in Canada until he was twenty and then migrated to Grand Rapids, Michigan, which was then known as the furniture capital of the world. In 1900, he married Clara Alice Speare, a Methodist from Preston, Ontario.[3]

After his wedding, John Gingrich was excommunicated from Mennonism for marrying a non-Mennonite.[4] Back in Grand Rapids, where there was no Mennonite congregation, John Gingrich joined the Fountain Street Baptist Church. "Its minister was one who made of his sermons virtual commentaries on current events," Gingrich remembered. "The services were followed by group discussions, held with the most seriously interested members of the congregation under the designation of Classes in Applied Christianity, and these too, my father joined, as earnest discussions always interested him."[5] His wife did not regularly attend church after she moved to the United States.

John Gingrich's first job in Grand Rapids was working on a throne sent by the residents of western Michigan to Queen Wilhelmina of Holland for her coronation. Following that he worked as a skilled craftsman for a number of furniture factories, including the Michigan Chair Company and the Sligh Furniture Company.[6] The best description of Grand Rapids in those days, disguised as Mill Center, is from Arnold Gingrich's autobiographical novel, *Cast Down the Laurel*, published in 1935:

The population at that time was about one hundred twenty thousand, of who [sic] twelve hundred knew all about each other and nothing about the other one hundred eighteen thousand eight hundred. . . . The town's aristocracy was one of industry ahead of trade, and of robbery ahead of either. Half the timber in the old days belonged to the government and half to those early settlers who happened to be on hand to claim it. Of these the more astute managed, by hook or by crook, to get out of remitting the government's share, and out of the margin came great fortunes. . . . Next after lumber came furniture, for which the town acquired a certain kind of fame, comparable to that of Sheffield for steel, Chicago for hogs. . . . If you or any of your family were connected, however remotely, with one of the town's many furniture factories, you were a person. You were, that is, if your connection lay through the office. If it led to the factory entrance you were a number on a time card—an anonymity as complete as a convict's, and one that your wife and your sons and daughters shared with you. . . . Here was one place in the land of the free where the meaning of democracy was not only never clear but never contemplated. Spiritually, intellectually, culturally, socially, you arrived at your station by birth and you stayed there, or if you changed it you did it out of town, and the change would never be recognized back home.[7]

Two histories of Michigan confirm Gingrich's observations. According to Willis Frederick Dunbar, "[Grand Rapids] seems to have possessed no particular advantage for furniture manufacturing. . . . [Its development] appears to be due to the businessmen who located there, their inventiveness, and the skilled craftsmen they attracted."[8] And in a history of the state written under the auspices of the Works Progress Administration, "The practice—now illegal—of importing from abroad what amounted to indentured labor, coupled with substandard wages and hours, caused an accumulation of grievances among the industry's thousands of workers."[9]

By 1903, when Arnold Gingrich was born, woodcarving was on

its way to extinction. In a few years it would be little more than a relic from the less technological days of the nineteenth century. In place of individual craftsmanship, machines made furniture much cheaper and faster than a man could. In the face of this technology, Gingrich's father remained a craftsman and never became a factory worker. But remaining true to his craft caused employment difficulties, as Gingrich remembered later:

> It was the increasing frequency with which he found himself laid off for a week or more at a time that led him to take the civil service examination, to see if he couldn't piece out the slack times in the furniture factories with some assignments to railway mail runs as a substitute. Since even the regular clerks were employed on a basis of a week off for every week on the road, so arduous were the hours during their periods of duty, it appeared to him an ideal combination of callings, and so it subsequently proved, for almost another decade, when the demand for hand-carved furniture petered out entirely.[10]

Gingrich said his father was a timid unassertive man. His mother, he writes in his memoir, *Toys of a Lifetime*, was just the opposite. "She is alleged to have smuggled out no less sizable an object than a kitchen stove, disassembled it is true, past the customs between Sarnia, Ontario, and Port Huron, Michigan, by the simple expedient of stowing it beneath her feet and covering it with her voluminous skirt."[11]

Except for Sundays at the Fountain Road Baptist Church, and an occasional trip on the mail train between Grand Rapids and Chicago, Gingrich seems to have spent more time with his mother than his father. And, apparently, it was she who gave him his early interest in clothes, music, and literature.

One night in November, when he was eight years old, Gingrich and his mother were waiting for a streetcar at the corner of Lyon and Monroe, in front of Friedrich's Music Store. He looked through the plate-glass window and fell in love with a red violin with shiny black pegs, resting in an opened green-lined case. The violin cost twenty dollars, and Gingrich pleaded for it, pressing his nose against the shop window.[12] His parents didn't get him that one, but less than a month later they got him a better one for fifty dollars and gave it to him as a ninth birthday present. "I thought it was the most beautiful thing I had ever seen, let alone been allowed to pick up and touch and call my own," he wrote in his memoirs. But Gingrich and the violin were not to make sweet music together. He said he knew he was bad at arithmetic, but added that it never occurred to him that a lack of mathematical ability could signal monumental failure as a musician. He took lessons for fifty cents a week and went from teacher to teacher. "I was to the fiddle as a mired car is to mud—the more you try to work it out the more hopelessly you bog it down. My playing a passage badly was bad enough. But playing it over a thousand times only made it that much worse, like spinning the wheels of a car that has lost traction, and only digs itself deeper with every turn. . . . Just before my sixteenth birthday, I finally faced up to the fact, that had been evident to everybody else since my ninth, that I had in me none of the makings of any sort of violinist. So I hung up the fiddle and bow," he wrote in *Toys of a Lifetime*.

At some point in his childhood, the year is uncertain, he was forced to remain in bed for nine months with a leg injury. While he recovered, his mother brought him library books, and by the end of that year he claims he had read eleven hundred volumes. It was the beginning of a lifelong interest in literature.[13]

Until he was eight years old, Gingrich, whose family was not among the Grand Rapids elite he described in *Cast Down the Laurel*, wore clothes handmade by his mother. But when he decided he wanted a Norfolk suit—a style that featured a square front with three buttons on the jacket and deep-cuffed trousers—he had seen in the Sears, Roebuck catalogue, she discovered his tastes had become too complicated for her sewing abilities and sent away for it. The order was delayed, and Gingrich pined for the suit the way other boys would yearn for a bicycle. "[That] shows that my interest in clothes was early and intense, as I can't imagine that most kids would make such an unholy fuss over the mere matter of whether or not a suit was delivered on a given day," he wrote in his memoirs.[14]

At age twelve, in the summer of 1916, Gingrich went to work in the clothing business. He applied for a job as a "boy" at Mackenzie-Bostock-Monroe in the carriage-trade district of upper Monroe. They weren't interested. Neither were the owners at A. May & Sons on working-class lower Monroe. Considering his father's bouts with unemployment and the fact that his younger brother, Robert John, had been born three years earlier, a job with an additional income was something the family needed.[15] With the haberdashers not hiring twelve-year-olds, he settled for working as a delivery boy for the E. R. Lee Paper Company on Lyons Street, overlooking the Grand River.[16] "All I had to do was sit there, at the back of the warehouse where there was a table and chair and wait for orders to come in for me to deliver," Gingrich wrote. "And the boss had no objection to my reading to pass the time. . . . I read all of Mark Twain [and] most of Henry James."[17] He worked there for three summers and then took a job at Collat's, a cut-rate men's store that hired him for three dollars and fifty cents a week, fifty cents more than he'd been getting at the paper company.[18]

When Gingrich entered Central High School in Grand Rapids in 1918, literature continued as one of his great passions. He was particularly attracted to Ezra Pound, e. e. cummings, and F. Scott Fitzgerald. His attraction to Fitzgerald might have been because the writer was a fellow midwesterner who left home and found fame.[19] Years later, he remembered his love for Fitzgerald's writing:

> In Central High School in Grand Rapids in 1920 I remember confiding in Margaret Robinson, a young teacher of French, to the extent of telling her how F. Scott Fitzgerald, in *This Side of Paradise*, had been able to read my inmost thoughts and ascribe them to a fictional character called Amory Blaine, and how dashed I was when she said she was sure that lots of boys had felt that way about lots of books, ever since books began to be printed, though it was the best excuse she'd heard that year for why one boy was behind in his written French exercises.[20]

He was on the yearbook literary staff in high school and wrote for a newspaper called *The Breezy Gazette*.[21] He also made plans for a magazine called *The St. Vitus Rag*, which was to be "a Dizzy dumping ground of dynamic discourses and wobbly witticism."[22] In his senior year he was elected class wit, and under his picture in his senior yearbook there is a quotation from Thackeray: "I have a natural taste for books."[23]

Literature may have been Gingrich's most obvious passion during his high school years, but he didn't spend all his spare time reading. He became enamored of Helen Mary Rowe, a classmate. Like Arnold, Helen Mary was a member of the Fountain Street Baptist Church, but socially she was far above the son of a woodcarver-turned-postman. Her father, William S. Rowe, was president and general manager of the Valley City Milling Company. He was also president and manager of the East Side Water Company, president of the Herkimer Hotel Company, vice-president of the Globe Realty Company, president of the West Michigan Millers Association, director of the Michigan Millers' Mutual Fire Insurance Company, the Furniture City Realty Company, the Holten Tire Company, and the Michigan Manufacturers Association. He was a member of the Highland Country Club and the Peninsular Club, not to mention the De Molai Commandery, the Knights Templars, the Saladin Shrine, the Kiwanis Club, the Chamber of Commerce, and the Fountain Street Baptist Church. William Rowe had inherited the milling business from his father, who started it before the turn of the century, and he lived in the suburbs.[24] Yet Helen's was not an ideal family. Her parents were divorced.

When Gingrich graduated from high school in 1920 he had some of the trappings of a midwestern sophisticate. He was an incompetent violinist, but he knew music. He knew books and authors and was a reader of the *Dial*, one of the country's best-known intellectual magazines.[25] He had worked on school newspapers and the literary section of the yearbook.[26] And he had been named class wit. Add to that his courtship of one of the town's budding high-society dames. His sophistication, as Harold Hayes said later, was self-made, not inherited.[27] When he remembered his youth, it was not always as a young intellectual; he never forgot his working-class origins. On the flyleaf of *Cast Down The Laurel*, Alfred Knopf, the publisher, announced a forthcoming book by Gingrich, *Happily Forever After: A Novel of Poverty in Youth*.[28] The novel was never published, but its title shows that Gingrich was not unaware of his circumstances.

Helen Mary Rowe left for the University of Wisconsin that fall.[29] Gingrich stayed home and entered Grand Rapids Junior College, where his writing abilities exempted him from two semesters of English composition.[30] A year later, in 1921, he transferred to the University of Michigan. His educational opportunities were certainly better on the campus at Ann Arbor than at the junior college in Grand Rapids, but staying in school would be a financial as well as an academic struggle. He worked in the University library fifty-four hours a week, bartered advertising copy for clothes at a campus men's store, and spent his summers selling Wear-Ever aluminum pots and pans to housewives in the Grand Haven and Spring Lake areas.[31]

Arnold's life was not all a grind. On weekends he would make the two-hundred-mile trip from Ann Arbor to Madison, Wisconsin, to see Helen Mary. He probably rode either the bus or train, since he didn't get his first car until 1929. Of course, Helen Mary may have done some of the traveling. Their passion was evidently intense: on October 24, 1924, fifteen months after Helen Mary's father died, the couple was married in Ypsilanti, Michigan, about twenty miles from Ann Arbor.[32] The service was conducted "by a justice of the peace in a simple ceremony interrupted only briefly by a farmer who wanted to sell the justice some potatoes."[33] After the marriage the couple separated—Helen Mary went back to the University of Wisconsin and Arnold continued his studies at the University of Michigan. They were both graduated in 1925. Arnold took his magna cum laude degree and his Phi Beta Kappa key and went looking for work.[34]

For reasons involving either finance, social status, or just to keep his mother-in-law happy, Arnold and Helen Mary decided to keep their marriage a secret. Of course, in the early part of this century, undergraduate students who married were often kicked out of school, and that may have been a factor as well. After graduation, Arnold approached Mrs. Rowe, whom he called "an ardent D.A.R.," and asked her permission to marry Helen Mary.

> We knew that if we could persuade my then mother-in-law to let us get married at all, we would have to do it her way this time, and meet whatever conditions she imposed for what would undoubtedly be a much more elaborate wedding. When the subject was first broached, my then mother-in-law, while unenthusiastic, was not adamant

in her opposition to the idea. . . . She imposed her first consideration, as a prerequisite before she would even entertain any further the idea of our getting married. This was that I must have a job, paying fifty dollars a week.[35]

Gingrich headed for Chicago and started pounding the pavements, looking for a job as a writer. He was hired thirty-seven times between the end of June and the first of August but he never took the job because the starting salary was always less than the amount he needed to get publicly married. The best offer he got was from the *Chicago Herald-Examiner,* the Hearst morning newspaper in that city. The paper offered to pay him $37.50, but that was $12.50 short of what he needed, so he turned it down. Finally, he went to the Osten Advertising Agency and volunteered to work for free. Gingrich's logic, he wrote in *Toys of a Lifetime,* was that most potential employers wouldn't hire a man without experience, and, since he had none, he could gain it from the agency and then find a job paying $50 a week. He worked at Osten designing layouts and writing copy while he ate for a dime a day on day-old buns from a Clark Street bakery and stayed for $2.50 a week in a makeshift cellar room on Superior Street. He worked for Osten for several months, at one time squandering half of his remaining ten dollars on a George Moore first edition, possibly the first volume in what would become a large rare-book collection. Then Gingrich found a job that paid the salary he needed. It was as director of the advertising services department for *Rock Products,* the journal of the Non-Metallic Mineral Industries. Gingrich conned the president of the company, W. D. Calendar, into thinking he was an engineer, and he was hired.

Although the American advertising industry is usually associated with Madison Avenue in New York, a Chicago agency, Lord and Thomas, helped to change the nature of the business. The man who made the change was A. D. Lasker, who made copywriting, not sloganeering, the central focus of advertisements. Lasker and two copywriters, John E. Kennedy and Claude C. Hopkins, operated under the theory that advertising was salesmanship in print. Lasker's domination of the advertising business in the Midwest began in 1899. He is said to have ignored stacks of marketing research statistics and instead concentrated on what the advertising said. His clients included

The American Cereal Company, maker of Quaker Oats; Cotosuet, a Swift and Company shortening; Dr. Shoop's restorative; and Schlitz Beer. All were midwestern companies.[36] When Gingrich decided to go for the higher wages of advertising rather than the adventure of journalism, he probably did not feel he was turning down creativity; Chicago advertising, to a greater extent than what was being produced in New York, emphasized writing. In New York, the account executive was king; in Chicago, the copywriter had that role.

Arnold Gingrich and Helen Mary Rowe were married in public in the spring of 1926. How much of a dowry she had, or whether the public wedding was just for social reasons, is unclear. When her father's $175,000 estate was settled shortly after he died, the will left her only $500.[37] How much money her mother had independently, either through family connection or as a settlement or alimony from Rowe, remains a mystery. But there was apparently some money involved. In a 1938 interview with *Scribner's* magazine, David Smart, the publisher of *Esquire*, referred to Gingrich as "the only rich genius we have." And Gingrich says his wife's remark, "Oh, Arnold only married me for his money," was "the sharpest thing said about me."[38]

Gingrich at least had enough money to invest in the Penguin Cafe with poet Kenneth Rexroth. Gingrich met Rexroth in 1926 and suggested the name for the new bohemian restaurant. A little later, Gingrich and a Chicago photographer, Fritz Roder, became the sole owners of the place, but it closed after only a few months.[39]

At about the same time as his public wedding, after more than a year writing ads for *Rock Products*, Gingrich saw a help wanted ad for a copywriter for B. Kuppenheimer & Company, a major manufacturer of men's clothing, and applied for the job. He was hired for sixty-five dollars a week.[40] At Kuppenheimer, Gingrich rose rapidly. Eighteen months after being hired in the spring of 1926, he had received three ten-dollar-a-week raises and was acting as advertising manager.[41]

Also during this time, his first son, Rowe, was born, on November 23, 1927.[42] What Gingrich could not have known was that as different as his life was from his days in Grand Rapids, it was about to make an even bigger change.

Enter David Smart.

"David Smart was a son of a bitch," said Martin Mayer, a former music critic and copy editor for *Esquire*. "He was a nasty fellow, a bully." He "had the aggressiveness that seems second nature to short men and . . . had a low boiling point," Gingrich wrote.[43] One of the best portraits of Smart is Gingrich's description of him at a party for Alfred Knopf, the New York publisher:

> Well, jeez, [Smart said] he prints all those beautiful books, and I was thinking if I could get on the right side of him maybe he'd sell me forty-three yards of them, only all different titles—I mean only one of each, you understand,—to fill the shelves in the new Apart(ment) . . . in the Drake Towers. . . . So all was going well, and Dave for once was not saying, "Now lemme tell ya how to run your business, Mr. Knopf" (or Picasso or Duveen or Lasker, Hearst or Mellon or Ford or Edison, hell it wouldn't have mattered which, including Diaghilev or Chaplin or Paderewski or Kreisler, he'd have told 'em all how).[44]

David Archibald Smart, like Gingrich, was the son of a craftsman. He was born in Omaha, Nebraska, on October 4, 1892. His father, Louis, was a Russian immigrant who came to Omaha, married Mary Aronson, and worked as a barber and voice teacher. David Smart moved to Chicago with his parents and his younger brothers and sisters—Alfred, John, Flossie, and Vera—when he was a small boy. He attended Crane Technical High School for a short time but left without graduating. The Smarts lived on Chicago's West Side, in the old Jewish neighborhood. The area contained some of the worst slums in Chicago and was a place "to settle upon arrival . . . and leave as soon as possible."[45]

Although ethnic neighborhoods may conjure up images of pushcart vendors and small business owners, most of the people on the West Side worked in factories. If there was one industry that dominated the neighborhood, it was clothing manufacturing. Most of the shops were small in scale, owned by someone who lived in the neighborhood, but two of the country's major manufacturers of men's clothes—B. Kuppenheimer and Hart Schaffner and Marx—were there as well. Kuppenheimer's factory opened in Chicago in 1876 after its founder, Bernard Kuppenheimer, moved his retail clothing business from Terre Haute, Indiana. Three years before Kuppenheimer moved to Chicago, Harry Hart and Brother opened a retail men's clothing store on State Street in Chicago. Out-of-town retailers routinely purchased suits from Hart to take home and sell, and by 1879, Hart, along with a brother-in-law and a distant relative, formed Hart Schaffner and Marx. It became the largest manufacturer of men's clothing in the United States and was the first men's clothing company to use national advertising. In 1890 it also became the first company to develop a national brand name for men's suits. That same year, Kuppenheimer opened its first advertising department.[46] New York may have been the center of the nation's garment industry, but in the manufacturing and merchandising of men's clothes, Chicago was also a leader.

Smart got his first job while he was still in high school. He worked as a hat salesman in a nationally known men's clothing store called The Hub (later Lytton's), where he enchanted customers with a trick that involved somersaulting a hat over his arm to make a crease.[47] In 1911 he left high school and The Hub and went to work as a classified advertising salesman for the *Chicago Tribune*. He developed the idea of selling classified space to small businessmen who couldn't afford the more expensive display rates. His idea worked, and he became a star salesman whose commissions were so high he was given a salary, which meant more security but less cash. Smart was interested in money, so in 1914 he left to form his own advertising agency. He was successful enough to send his brother, Alfred, through the University of Illinois.

His career was interrupted when he served in Germany in World War I as a private in the field artillery. Smart was wounded slightly and returned to Chicago, where he began investing in the commodity market. He made $750,000 speculating on sugar, then lost all but $50,000 of it in a market crash. In 1921 he went back to advertising. With his brother Alfred, who gave up a job as an engineer with the City of Chicago's Sanitary Department to join him as secretary-treasurer, he started the David A. Smart Publishing Company.[48] In the beginning, the company didn't really publish anything. It made promotional items—posters, booklets, calendars, memo pads—for banks, haberdashers, and furniture stores. During those years Smart developed a business strategy that he used through the formation of *Esquire*. He would sell the advertising booklets and brochures he offered before printing them, thereby assuring himself a profit before the presses ever turned.

During those years, Smart moved his family from the West Side to a number of houses and apartments, finally settling them on Sheridan Avenue on Chicago's Near North Side. Although he was something of a rake, he lived at home with his parents until he was in his forties. He dreamed of owning horses, and, Gingrich remembers, he talked in Time-speak, thinking that imitating the convoluted prose of Henry Luce's newsmagazine would mark him as a sophisticate.[49]

In 1926 Smart formed a partnership with William Hobart Weintraub, a traveling salesman for the H. O. Reno Company, a clothing manufacturer, and formed the Men's Wear Service Corporation. At first, the new company published *The Man of Today*, a trade magazine for clothing stores. In December of that year Smart and Weintraub changed the name of the publication to *Gentlemen's Quarterly*, and it became a catalogue for haberdashers. It is not surprising that these two men would turn to catalogues as sales tools. America's two largest retailers, Sears, Roebuck and Montgomery Ward, were both in Chicago, and both successful because of their catalogues.

In some ways, Smart and Weintraub were alike. They were both under five foot nine, both aggressive salesmen who spoke the language of the street, and both aspired to the upper rungs of society. Weintraub, who had dropped out of college at the beginning of World War I, affected a college background by wearing a gold football on his vest chain. A close look would reveal that the bauble was from Great Lakes Naval Air Training Station, not an institution of higher learning. Smart had light, curly hair and was slender and blue-eyed, while Weintraub was dark and stocky. Neither man liked the other very much. The partnership continued to exist only because the money rolled in. By 1929 Weintraub had moved to New York to handle the firm's advertising sales, while Smart and Gingrich remained in Chicago.

Offering catalogues for men's clothes was a new idea. Until *Gentlemen's Quarterly* was published, most catalogues published were for women. There seemed to be little interest in fashion among men. *Vanity Fair* published an occasional column, "What the Well-Dressed Man Will Wear," but that was about it. *Gentlemen's Quarterly* was disguised as a magazine, however, and was given free to charge-account customers at men's stores throughout the country. The name of the store was imprinted on all the copies of *Gentlemen's Quarterly* a company bought. The editorial content was minimal, but it was a precursor to *Esquire* in its emphasis on articles for affluent or aspiring men. The magazine featured stories like "The United Hunts" and "The Princeton House Parties," along with articles about the proper care of clothes and the proper coordination of colors.[50]

According to Gingrich,

> This was an era when presidents were photographed on trout streams wearing vests and derbies, when Dressing for the Occasion was only an advertising slogan and not the actual and universal practice it has become. . . . *Gentlemen's Quarterly* was forcing men's stores into the unaccustomed role of actively stimulating their customers' hitherto unsuspected wants, as opposed to catering passively to their routine needs. And in order to do that they had to buy the new items of fashion that were featured in *Gentlemen's Quarterly*, that were of a sophisticated and avant-garde nature in total contrast to their normal stocks of goods on hand.[51]

To get *Gentlemen's Quarterly*, the men's stores had to agree to stock all the merchandise advertised in the catalogue and pay two hundred dollars per thousand copies. By early December 1928, the company was shipping the catalogues to more than two hundred men's stores around the country. *Gentlemen's Quarterly* used four-color printing, had twenty-four pages per issue, and printed more than 180,000 copies per issue.

Soon the company began putting out additional catalogues and selling them to different chains of men's stores. Businesses featuring Hart Schaffner and Marx merchandise got *Club and Campus*; another one was in the works for stores that sold Fashion Park Clothes. The Men's Wear Service Corporation's copywriter, Dale

Fisher, left the firm in 1928, and Smart began casting about for a replacement. Three different people gave him Gingrich's name and, according to *Nothing But People*, Gingrich's book about the early days at *Esquire*, told him that the young Kuppenheimer ad man could write "broad-A English." Gingrich liked his job at Kuppenheimer, liked the annual salary of sixty-five hundred dollars and the apartment in suburban Evanston it afforded him. But he was writing radio scripts for Chicago stations and stories for the New York pulp magazines *Breezy Stories*, *Droll Stories*, and *Pep* for extra money, now that there was a baby. And he and his wife were both collecting first editions. So he listened to Smart, played hard to get, and then finally took the job in December 1928. From the beginning, Gingrich had done more than take a new job; he had joined a family. Smart's employees included not only his brother Alfred, and another brother, John, but also the husbands of his two sisters, and a cousin or two. But Gingrich never seemed to mind. In fact, he seemed happy to have been adopted by the corporation and its system of paternalism.

> I was simply the most local [employee]. My salary, or my "earnings," which I never knew anything about until they materialized on occasions when I could appreciate them most, were really none of my business. My salary was whatever Dave said it was. From days of signing that first . . . contract with him, I never again discussed salary with him, but only listened every time he told me, as he often did, that I was earning more than I thought I was. . . . Never having put a penny of my own into the business, I figured that any part of it that he said was mine was pure manna, and as such was nothing ever to be questioned or discussed and certainly not argued about. If for reasons of his own he wanted to say that it was one thing when I thought it was another, then that was his right, as indeed it was his right at any time to say it was nothing, for that's what it had been in the beginning and hence could certainly be again.[52]

By 1929, the company was publishing three other catalogues— *The Observer*, *The Etonian*, and, seasonally, *Gifts for a Gentleman*.

Gingrich edited them all, using a different name—J. V. Arnold for *Gentlemen's Quarterly,* Arnold Gingrich for *Club and Campus,* and Wakefield Speare, a combination of his mother's and grandmother's maiden names, for *The Observer.* In 1929 Smart gave Gingrich a Ford as a bonus. But before any gentleman had a chance to dream about the items offered in the Christmas catalogue, the bottom fell out of the stock market in October 1929. And when it did, it took the bottom out of the clothing market as well. Smart tried to make up for the failing catalogues with a scheme that involved candid pictures of opening-night Broadway dandies in their new finery. The pictures were sent by wire, using a technology newspapers had begun using in 1927, to clothing stores all over the country and were put in shop windows to show the local clotheshorses what was fashionable in New York. That was supposed to make them buy the same outfit for themselves.[53] But *Men's Wear,* the trade magazine put out by the Fairchild Company, a trade-magazine corporation founded in Chicago in 1892 that relocated to New York in 1900 and issued specialized business magazines in dozens of fields, scoffed at Smart's scheme. Under a headline that called Smart and company, "Fair Weather Fashion Experts," *Men's Wear* insinuated that the pictures were staged with models substituted for the actual theater crowd.[54]

Smart, Weintraub, and Gingrich decided to retaliate by putting out a trade magazine to compete with Fairchild's *Men's Wear.* It would be modeled on Henry Luce's *Fortune,* a sumptuous monthly magazine that used some of the nation's best artists and writers to celebrate the American corporation. The Gingrich/Smart magazine would be a quarterly called *Apparel Arts;* the first issue appeared September 15, 1931, with a press-run of 7,500.[55] It had 148 pages, including 90 full-page advertisements and a feature on Brooks Brothers men's store. Although enough advertising had been sold to assure a profit before the press turned, the editorial content was higher than in the previous fashion booklets. One issue, for example, had a photo essay by Margaret Bourke-White on sweatshops in New York. Another included reproductions of drawings by popular artist Joseph Christian Leyendecker. *Time* wrote about the appearance of *Apparel Arts,* particularly about how it imitated *Fortune. Apparel Arts* had, *Time* said, "same page size (11^1/$_2$" by 14") as *Fortune,* similar paper stocks (antique and coated), with colored cartographs and modernist photographs in the *Fortune* manner of stylized detail. It even carries its name and volume number on the binding in white as *Fortune* does."[56]

On the masthead, Gingrich was listed as "Editor." It was the first time he'd ever had that title. Until then, he'd just been a copywriter. "The result," he wrote in *Nothing But People*, "was a truly untrade-paperish trade paper, and one that none of us would have had the wit to plan. Instead of the dull and dry articles, of a really reportorial and informational character, that we had hoped to obtain but couldn't because everything went wrong, we had a lively book of a much more inspirational type, with fictional techniques employed, like a sauce, to cover up the fact that we didn't have much to offer in the way of factual data."[57]

The magazine, which acknowledged that it was a copy of *Fortune*, became popular not only as a trade publication but also as a catalogue for men's stores. Instead of having to keep all the merchandise on hand, as they did in the *Gentlemen's Quarterly* days, a store could show a customer a copy of *Apparel Arts* and then offer to order anything that wasn't in stock. In the Depression days, this retail mail-order catalogue had an appeal to both the merchant and the customer. Between 1929 and 1933 the dollar volume of retail sales in men's stores had dropped by 49 percent. The number of men's stores throughout the country dropped by 40 percent, and 8 percent of them went bankrupt.[58] By the second issue, it became apparent that the magazine was being used as a sales aid, displayed in special metal racks in men's stores.[59]

Just over a year later, shortly after Thanksgiving of 1932, C. F. Peters, a freelance fashion artist who worked occasionally for *Apparel Arts,* told Smart, Weintraub, and Gingrich that Rogers Peet, a major New York men's store, would be interested in reviving the pre-Depression fashion booklets. Only this time, the artist said, since it was the Depression, maybe the store could sell the booklets for a dime, rather than distributing them for free. Gingrich grabbed a paste pot and scissors and began putting together fashion layout sheets based on the pages of *Apparel Arts.* Weintraub started estimating advertising revenue and printing costs. Smart shouted ideas for the nonfashion editorial content—Hemingway on fishing, Bobby Jones on golf, Jack Dempsey on boxing. The more they talked, the more expensive the proposed new magazine became. Its cover price rose from a dime to half a dollar. First it was called *Trend,* but a Washington patent attorney said that name was taken. So were their next three choices, *Stag, Beau,* and *Trim.* Finally, and unenthusiastically, it was titled *Esquire,* after they noticed a letter from their attorney addressed to "Arnold Gingrich, Esq." The nameplate for the magazine was an artistic modification of Gingrich's handwriting.

3 Men About Town

hen *Esquire* was first published, *Time* called it a *Vogue* for men.[1] There was a great difference, however. *Vogue*, which started publication in 1892, was targeted at an elite market of New Yorkers. It celebrated "the ceremonial side of life" and counted among its backers Cornelius Vanderbilt, Mrs. Stuyvesant Fish, and Mrs. William D. Sloan.[2] In 1909, the magazine was bought by Condé Nast, who had been advertising manager at *Collier's*, but he never planned for it to appeal to a mass market. Much of the magazine's content, like the proposed *Esquire*, would be fashion. There was no need, however, to pretend that *Vogue* was something besides a fashion magazine or to expand its appeal to the middle classes. To be successful for the market its publishers had selected, *Esquire* would have to do both.

Conventional wisdom of the day was that a fifty-cent consumer magazine for American men would never work, even if it were frankly bawdy. And with women controlling 85 percent of the purchase of all consumer goods, there would be no market for national advertisers.[3] The *Esquire* founders disagreed. The magazine, initially planned as a quarterly, was presold to one thousand haberdashers—each took an agreed-upon quantity—guaranteeing a circulation of one hundred thousand and a profit before the press ever turned. But there was still a nagging problem: would anybody read it?

Although Smart, Gingrich, and Weintraub had been successful with fashion booklets and a trade magazine, all three doubted that enough men would buy a magazine devoted exclusively to clothes to make it profitable. There was good reason for their doubts. Men didn't think about style. That was confirmed in 1942 when Hart Schaffner and Marx, in cooperation with the Psychological

Corporation of America, surveyed the buying habits of the American male clothing customer. Fit and quality of material were men's first concerns; style was third.[4]

When men did think about style, it brought their masculinity into question. As M. M. Lebensburger wrote in 1939 in *Selling Men's Apparel Through Advertising,*

> Although men wanted to be "in style" and approve of style as an idea, there is in the male make-up an instinct which resists any outward manifestation of this feeling. . . . Because women are so obviously and notoriously interested in personal appearance and style there is a feeling common among men that any demonstration of this same interest on their part is an indication of effeminacy. An outward manifestation of distaste for style or indifference to style is, therefore considered a mark of masculinity.[5]

Beginning in the 1920s, according to John D'Emilio and Estelle Freedman, gender played a continuing role in shaping an individual's sense of sexual meaning and determining how the erotic remained attached to concepts of gender.[6] In other words, women worried about style; men didn't. And if a man worried about style it made him appear more effeminate and brought his masculine sexuality into question. It was a matter of homophobia. No man wanted to be seen as less masculine than another, for fear he would be labeled a sissy. And fashion in those times was thought to be a sissy's concern. Or, as Arnold Gingrich put it, the new magazine needed "something . . . substantial enough to deodorize the lavender [or, in today's terms, gay] whiff coming from the mere presence of fashion pages."[7] To eliminate that whiff, Gingrich devised an editing method that, as he would say later, was a lot like a three-ring circus.[8] Gingrich's three rings were fashion, off-beat masculine writing, and sex. And all three rings were to be hairy chested.

For masculinity, there was no hairier literary chest than Ernest Hemingway's. He was a renowned tough-guy writer, the inventor of that American style, as a matter of fact, and his best-selling novels, *The Sun Also Rises* and *A Farewell to Arms,* had made him world-famous. A former journalist, he wrote about hunting and fishing as well as bullfighting. If anyone could sweep the smell of lavender from the pages of the new fashion magazine, Hemingway could. And Gingrich had a scheme to hire him.

Since college days, Gingrich had been a rare-book collector. He specialized in first editions by Ernest Hemingway, F. Scott Fitzgerald, and John Dos Passos. His wife collected Ring Lardner. But Gingrich's fascination with Hemingway, another midwesterner, went beyond first editions. He had copies of the school paper and class yearbook Hemingway had worked on in high school in Oak Park, Illinois and had been writing fan letters to the author's home in Key West.[9] "Gingrich was an ardent book collector who had written to Ernest," wrote Hemingway biographer Carlos Baker, "asking him to autograph a copy of *Death in the Afternoon*. Ernest had advised Gingrich not to be 'spooked' by the reviewers' criticisms of the book. Old Papa said he still felt pretty good."[10]

Gingrich's collecting led him to write to Captain L. H. Cohn, who owned The House of Books, a New York rare-book store, and ask him to be on the lookout for rare Hemingway editions. On March 4, 1933, the day Roosevelt declared a bank holiday, Gingrich was in New York, where he got an offer from Cohn to sell him a first edition of *Three Stories and Ten Poems*. Only 350 copies of that book, which was published in Paris in 1923 by Contact Editions, were printed. Cohn said Gingrich could have one for seventy-five dollars.[11] The young editor hurried over to The House of Books and there, in the flesh, was Hemingway. Here is Gingrich's memory of that meeting:

> He quickly agreed, at least in principle, to my suggestion that he do us some kind of sporting letter covering his different outdoor activities, and then went on to offer suggestions about other people I ought to try to get, and in several instances said, "and you can say I sent you." . . . On the way downtown he spelled out what he meant by agreement in principle to write for us. . . . "I don't care how much or how little you pay," he said and then corrected himself immediately, "Hell yes, I do care, but the big stuff I can always get by selling stories, and you and I are talking about journalism. Let's say you pay fifty bucks or let's say you pay a hundred—or let's just say that what-

ever you pay, as your going rate, you pay me double . . . "
Right, I said, and we shook on it.[12]

That first meeting was described differently by Hemingway's biographer. "It was at Cohn's place of business that Ernest first met a
young Pennsylvania Dutchman named Arnold Gingrich. . . .
Gingrich was currently editing a trade journal called *Apparel Arts,*
with headquarters in Chicago. He thought Ernest 'a swell guy' and
was disappointed when he cut the interview short and rushed away
to catch his train to Virginia."[13] According to Baker, the offer to write
for the new magazine didn't come until weeks later.

> Arnold Gingrich had lately written Ernest about a new
> men's magazine, as yet unnamed, which would begin pub-
> lication in the fall. He wanted Ernest as a contributor, and
> would pay $250 apiece for short, nonfiction articles on
> hunting and fishing. The magazine would attempt to do
> for American men what *Vogue* was doing for the Ameri-
> can woman. Gingrich said Ernest need not worry about
> its quality. It was not going to be a sissy [homophobia
> again] journal. It would have "ample hair on its chest and
> adequate cojones [balls]." When Ernest promised to do
> some articles, Gingrich sent him a stylish blue shirt and
> a leather jerkin, culled from the clothing made available
> to the editor of *Apparel Arts* by various advertisers.[14]

Hemingway's association with *Esquire* continued through the
1930s. In all, he wrote for *Esquire* thirty-three times. Most of it was
journalism, but one contribution was "The Snows of Kilimanjaro,"
a short story that was a substitute for two of his journalistic pieces.
Gingrich also came through for the author in 1933 when Hemingway
needed $3,300 as a down payment for his fishing boat, the *Pilar.* The
editor charged the money as an advance against future contributions,
one of which was the famous short story. Later that year, after he
had taken delivery of the boat in Miami, Hemingway invited Gingrich
to Key West to go big-game fishing. Gingrich was supposed to bring
F. Scott Fitzgerald along, but Fitzgerald backed out, saying his mother
was ill. On the boat, among others, was John Dos Passos, who never

liked Gingrich much. Dos Passos recounted the adventure in a cable to Pauline Pfeiffer, Hemingway's second wife:

> [Gingrich] was in a trance. It was a world he'd never dreamed of. He was mosquito bitten, half seasick, scorched with sunburn, astonished, half scared, half pleased. It was as much fun to see Ernest play an editor as to see him play a marlin. Gingrich never took his fascinated eyes off Old Hem. Hem would reel in gently, letting his prey have plenty of line. The editor was hooked.[15]

Later, on a 1936 trip to Bimini to visit Hemingway, Gingrich met Jane Mason, a Hemingway groupie who had been the model for Margot Macomber in the short story "The Short Happy Life of Francis Macomber." It was an unflattering portrait—Mrs. Macomber shoots her husband. Gingrich and Mason began an affair that lasted, on and off, until 1955, when they were married.[16] So the Hemingway connection meant as much for Gingrich's personal life as it did for *Esquire*. In fact, David Smart considered Hemingway so valuable a contributor that in 1937 he gave the author one thousand shares of *Esquire* stock. But all that was in the future in 1933 when Hemingway agreed to become *Esquire*'s star contributor.

With Hemingway in his stable of writers, Gingrich started rounding up other authors, but it involved more than going door-to-door saying "Ernest sent me." Of course, using Hemingway's name had brought in some writers, but Gingrich, whose taste was for nonformula writing, got others by asking mass circulation magazines such as *The Saturday Evening Post* for manuscripts by famous authors that seemed too daring to use. The publishers sent them and Gingrich was able to get thousands of dollars' worth of stories for only hundreds. He also offered prompt payment, not a small inducement in the Depression.[17] The first issue included writing by Hemingway, John Dos Passos, William McFee, Erskine Caldwell, Manuel Komroff, Morley Callaghan, and Dashiell Hammett, plus pieces by Gene Tunney, Bobby Jones, and Benny Leonard.[18] Although *Esquire* may have rejected the star system when it came to its pictures of women, that was exactly what it used in pursuing literature. Little of what the magazine printed in its first few issues had lasting quality, but the names certainly did. For decades, *Esquire* would advertise the names of Pulitzer and Nobel prize winners who had appeared in the magazine's pages. In the beginning, Gingrich was paying for bylines, not quality. Later, the quality improved.

Considering that much of *Esquire*'s fiction came from rejection piles at other magazines, it's instructive to study what kind of stories other publishers didn't want by looking at their magazines and by studying issues of *Esquire*. *The Saturday Evening Post*, even though it published fiction by Fitzgerald and Faulkner, wanted "wholesome" stories that would fit in with its business-oriented editorial policy and Norman Rockwell covers. *The New Yorker* was looking for sophisticated wit. *Vanity Fair*, under the editorship of Frank Crowninshield, was only interested in what concerned high society. *Scribner's*, *The Smart Set*, and *The American Mercury* were designed for intellectuals. Given those limitations, it's easy to see how Gingrich was able to pick up a lot of manuscripts at bargain prices. As one unnamed writer told *The Literary Digest,*

> When I have an idea which won't fit the formula of my regular market, I work it out and shoot it to *Esquire*. There's not much money in it—about $200 for a story which would have brought $1,500 had it fitted the requirements of any of the big national weeklies. But *Esquire* serves a useful function—helps to alleviate the pain of sticking to formula writing. Sometimes it's fun to let your hair down—slop over on the intellectual side, the bawdy side or what have you.[19]

And most writers liked Gingrich's editing philosophy—he who edits least edits best.

Understanding *Esquire*'s fiction requires an analysis of several issues of the magazine. In the October 1934 issue, for example, there are eleven short stories. "One Friend to Mourn," by Frederick Scribner, is about a funeral for an old farmer from the Midwest; "A Man from Vienna," by Donald Charles, is an international intrigue thriller that imagines Hitler's double; "The Love of a Jinx," by Edward L. McKenna, tells the story of a bad-luck carny; "Call Me Up," by Rion Bercovici, details love amidst the new urban morality of an open marriage; "The Horrible God," by Thomas Burke, is a horror story with a macabre, racist twist; "The Conqueror," by Knut Hamsun, is a sex story about a man who sees each new woman as a conquest; "The Belle Dame," by Myron Griffin, tells the story of a poor, broken young woman in New York; "A Pastoral Scene," by Louis Paul, is a tale of a vagrant traveling through the heartland of America; "The Little Japanese," by Pierre Mille, is an account of racism in attitudes about women; "Always Second," by Michael Fessier, is a ghost story about a race car driver in Italy; and "To What Red Hell," by Chester Himes, who was serving time in the Ohio State Penitentiary for armed robbery when this story was written, depicts prison life during a fire in the Big House.

Of the eleven stories, seven are either about low-life characters (prisoners, vagrants, carnival workers) or have sex as their theme. That explains the reaction of E. Purdy of Chicago, who wrote in "The Sound and the Fury," *Esquire*'s letters-to-the-editor column, "Perhaps you may some day find material about a fine person doing something pleasant."[20] Only the Himes story and, possibly, the ones by Louis Paul and Myron Griffin, have lasting literary value. The rest are standard magazine fare of the era. Most of them could fit into the mystery or supernatural pulp magazines of the decade. But these stories represent only a small portion of *Esquire*'s fiction in the thirties. During that decade the magazine carried between eight and ten short stories per issue. That totals about five hundred short stories, making *Esquire* one of the major fiction markets in the country. When you're publishing that much, not every story can be a literary gem. What is amazing is that so many were.

Essentially, what Gingrich wanted was fiction that was daring. Maybe the best example is "A Good Job Gone," a short story by Langston Hughes published in April 1934. It was a story about miscegenation—an aging white man-about-town has an affair with a Harlem beauty and then falls apart after it is over. Gingrich pushed the story with promotional ads months before it appeared. The ads in issues of *Esquire* preceding publication asked readers whether "this sordid tale of miscegenation—the kind of story no commercial magazine would touch with a ten-foot pole" should be published.[21] Apparently there were more letters for publication than against.

After Hemingway, the most prominent *Esquire* contributor in the 1930s was F. Scott Fitzgerald. He was hardly hairy chested, but Fitzgerald had been a literary hero of Gingrich's ever since the editor was in high school. During the magazine's first full year of publication, Fitzgerald became a regular contributor. It gave the author a regular source of money—although it wasn't much, only $250 a story—and he could count on Gingrich accepting anything he wrote. It also gave Fitzgerald a chance to appear in a magazine where Hemingway was the star writer. The two had been friends and rivals since they both lived in Paris in the 1920s.[22]

Fitzgerald's best-known contribution to *Esquire* was a 1936 series of three articles ("The Crack Up," "Pasting It All Together," and "Handle With Care") about his nervous breakdown. Fitzgerald had been receiving advances from Gingrich even though he had writer's block and hadn't written anything. Finally, the editor told Fitzgerald he had to have something to show the accountants. He suggested Fitzgerald use the automatic writing method advanced by Gertrude Stein—just write down anything that came into his head. What he wrote down was a long confessional that embarrassed Maxwell Perkins, his editor at Scribner's. Hemingway said "The Crack Up" showed Fitzgerald was cowardly, and John Dos Passos suggested he give up fiction and get a job as a reporter.[23]

A year later, Fitzgerald was writing screenplays in Hollywood. On a trip to Chicago with his lover and companion, the Hollywood columnist Sheilah Graham, he called Gingrich from his hotel, across the street from *Esquire*'s offices, and demanded that the editor come over. Gingrich arrived and found Fitzgerald reeling. He ordered a steak sandwich and a quart of coffee and tried to sober Fitzgerald up. But the writer refused to eat, so Gingrich cut the steak into small pieces and spoon-fed him like a child. Fitzgerald bit Gingrich's fingers. When he poured coffee into Fitzgerald's mouth, the writer spit it into the editor's face.[24] Gingrich had an enormous capacity for forgiveness; in 1939 *Esquire* published Fitzgerald's "Pat Hobby's Christmas Wish," the first in a series of seventeen Pat Hobby stories about a Hollywood hack writer. The stories continued in the magazine until July 1941, six months after Fitzgerald died. They were published as a book edited by Gingrich in 1962.

Now that he had acquired the fashion pages and literature contributors, Gingrich turned his eye toward sex. "Arnold kept wanting to find a girl," remembers Jerry Jontry, the former advertising director of *Esquire*. "And one day he's driving along Michigan Avenue in Chicago and he sees a billboard. And he said, 'now that's the kind of girl I want.' Of course she was completely out of proportion. So he found out that there was an artist at Ruth, Roff and Ryan, an old Chicago agency, who had done it. He was making all of twenty-five dollars a week."[25]

The artist who had painted that billboard for Atlas-Prager Near Beer was George Petty, a bear of a man who began his career doing freelance lettering for Chicago commercial art studios. He eventually moved up to airbrush work and prepared illustrations for mail-order catalogues, working over photographs of women in girdle and brassiere ads. It was the airbrush that gave these pictures an almost three-dimensional quality.

The airbrush was invented in 1893 by Charles L. Burdick, a professional inventor who also patented humidifying systems, coin counting and sorting machines, and a machine for folding banknotes. Burdick was an amateur watercolor artist, and he developed the airbrush as a method of applying one watercolor on top of another without disturbing the one already on paper.[26] In essence, the air brush works like a spray gun. It has a nozzle that sprays paint on a surface in a fine mist and is powered by compressed air. Initially, the airbrush was used to cover flaws in photographs. It was also used to add color tints to black and white pictures. And, beginning with *Esquire* and the illustrations created by Petty, it was used to create women men dream about. They soon became known as Petty Girls.

"Petty girls . . . were not real," write art historians Seng-gye Tombs Curtis and Christopher Hunt in their history of the airbrush. "They were attractive, inviting, and unattainable. The style . . . suggests a plastic-quasi-reality, a bedroom any man could escape to without a suggestion of the real world to bring him down to earth."[27] To Arnold Gingrich, the Petty Girls looked all smoothed out. *Time* said they seemed to be made of soft pink pastry. They were more accurately described by Reid Austin, who worked as assistant art director for *Playboy* and has written an unpublished biography of Petty; he said the Petty Girls were streamlined.

As is well known, streamlining became the dominant industrial design in America in the 1930s. Although streamlining goes back to the 1920s, it was early in the 1930s, just after the election of Franklin Roosevelt, that the first industrial stylists started to redesign America's consumer goods in a move to increase retail sales and help end the Depression. The shapes they used most often were characterized by rounded edges, smooth surfaces, and low profiles. Most people think of streamlining as a new design for railroad steam engines, for aircraft, for ocean liners. But it became an industrial design that also reshaped radios, refrigerators, even cigarette lighters. "Streamlining cleansed the surfaces of . . . two-dimensional ornamental patterns and directed attention to the plastic qualities of three-dimensional form," writes Donald J. Bush in *The Streamlined Decade*.[28] It was the shape of least resistance.

It was also the shape of the Petty Girl. Her form was half industrial (the air brush) and half artistic. And as much as she became a fantasy for many *Esquire* readers, she was also an industrial design. In most of Petty's paintings, the shoes and clothes of the girls are only sketched in, while the rest of the painting—the face and body—is completed. In some ways, the Petty Girls are like the drawings in *Esquire* by Alexis de Sakhnoffsky, the designer of the first streamlined Greyhound bus. De Sakhnoffsky's drawings were used to show how objects of everyday life could be made over in a new, sophisticated, streamlined model ("In this mad era," reads the copy for the de Sakhnoffsky feature in the October 1934 *Esquire*, "even drinking accessories, it seems, have aerodynamic lines.") Petty's paintings showed a design for a new streamlined woman—all smoothed out and conforming to the shape of least resistance. She was a new model, another reshaped consumer item like de Sakhnoffsky's wineglass with streamlined fins. And she was designed to make the older models look obsolete and to make consumers yearn for the new one.

Of course, Petty's Girls were not the first drawings of women to become national phenomena. In the 1890s, Charles Dana Gibson, an illustrator for *Life* magazine, became famous for his engravings of Gibson Girls. The women Gibson drew were tall, with athletic, not voluptuous figures. They were always ladies and somewhat, but not entirely, innocent. They were members of the social elite that included college women and social workers at settlement houses. But the Gibson Girls were always women of leisure. They did not drink or smoke, in contrast to their successors, the John Held, Jr., flappers. Held's girls were angular and scantily clad, a far cry from the rounded and demure Gibson Girls. The flapper was rooted in the speakeasy of Prohibition, the Charleston, the Blackbottom, and other dances of the Jazz Age—not in the aristocracy. She was a sign of a new American sensuality that had been awakened after World War I. The flapper was wild. The Gibson Girl, although she was threatening to older styles of women models which came largely from high society, was tame. Each represented her era, but by the 1930s and the Depression, the wildness of the twenties had calmed. America needed a new imaginary ideal woman. She arrived in the form of the streamlined Petty Girl who was part chorus girl, part kept woman, and always a flirt. The Gibson Girl was a part of high society, the Flapper ignored it, and the Petty Girl satirized it.

Petty's "girls" appeared regularly from the first issue of *Esquire* in 1933 until 1940. During the first year of the magazine's publication, they appeared only eight times, and in their early incarnation they were part of a cartoon. In the first issue a smooth but fully clad blonde, who looks a lot like Jean Harlow, sits on the lap of a bald gentleman with a white mustache. The Petty Girls may have come from the idea of Broadway chorines, but they looked like Hollywood, which used chorus girls as characters in a lot of movies. There was no caption; the picture itself was the joke. Later Petty Girls were captioned, however. Most of the "gag" lines for the early Petty cartoons were furnished by *Esquire*'s premier cartoonist, E. Simms Campbell. By mid-1935 the old man had vanished, and then, month by month, all props and background disappeared until the Petty Girl was left standing alone with a telephone. The phone became a device for a gag line supplied by the editorial department. The drawing did not assume the double-page gatefold size until December 1939. Petty had no contract with *Esquire*; he worked, initially, for one hundred dollars a picture. By 1939 his rate was up to one thousand dollars per illustration and he supplemented that with advertising contracts to draw women for Old Gold cigarettes and Jantzen swimwear.[29]

Gingrich scheduled cartoons as part of the magazine from the first days of planning. Running them in color was an accident, however. Originally, the magazine was to include only twenty-four pages of full color, but the sale of advertising was so good the number was raised to thirty-six.[30] So *Esquire* became the first American magazine to run full-page cartoons in color. Although *Esquire*'s literary quality is what it's remembered for now, when the magazine was first published the cartoons overshadowed everything else. In an introduction to *The Bedside Esquire*, a collection of writing that had appeared in the magazine, Gingrich said, "Sometimes this editor, weary of hearing the cartoons talked about as if they characterized the contents as a whole, has been tempted to term [the writing in the magazine] the Esquire Nobody Knows."[31]

One of the great discoveries Gingrich made for that first issue was an African American cartoonist, E. Simms Campbell (1906–1971), who helped set the tone for the magazine for the next two decades. Campbell, the son of an assistant high school principal, was born in St. Louis on January 2. His mother, an artist who painted with watercolors, noticed her son's artistic abilities when he was four years old. Campbell and his family moved to Chicago in 1920, when he was fourteen. He graduated from Englewood High School and then attended the University of Chicago for a while before switching to the Chicago Institute of Fine Art. He graduated and moved to New York, where he lived with an aunt on Edgecombe Avenue in Harlem. In New York, he studied under George Grosz at the Art Students League during the day. At night he drew for *College Comics*, a humor magazine.

Campbell was no stranger to the racial discrimination of the day. "Oh, I could always draw," he said in a 1966 interview, "but I was a failure as an artist 'til I became a successful dining car waiter."[32] In the 1920s he had drawn a few cartoons for *Judge, The New Yorker, Opportunity* (the magazine of the Urban League), and *Crisis* (the magazine of the NAACP).[33] Gingrich went to see Campbell on the recommendation of Russell Patterson, a Sunday supplement artist who was famous for his weekly drawings of women in the Ziegfeld tradition. Patterson turned down a chance to work for the new men's magazine because the pay was too low, but he recommended Campbell if Gingrich wouldn't "draw the color line."[34]

The young editor said he wouldn't. "And besides," Gingrich added, "what the hell, magazines weren't wired for sound, so drawings wouldn't carry any trace of any kind of accent."[35] Gingrich met

Campbell in Harlem at the home of the artist's aunt. He was astounded by what he saw and agreed to buy scores of cartoons. In one of them was the figure of a popeyed man with a walrus mustache; as the *Esquire* trademark, he became known as Esky. That character, usually in the form of a three-dimensional clay model made by Sam Berman, appeared for twenty years on the cover of every *Esquire* except the first.[36] In *Esquire* Campbell became famous for his cartoon series featuring a short, fat, white sultan and his harem of tall, beautiful, white women. The harem drawings suggested a fantasy world filled with wealth and sex. His work appeared in *Esquire* every month until his death in 1971. In 1943 he started a weekly cartoon series of beautiful women called *Cuties* that was syndicated by King Features for almost three decades. In 1957, he moved to Switzerland. "Out here . . . I can walk into any joint I want to and nobody starts looking as if they're thinking, 'Ugh, there's a nigger in here.' "[37]

It may be the writing that distinguishes *Esquire* from other magazines of the thirties when it is examined six decades after publication, but while it was on the newsstands, as I have said, it was the cartoons that had people talking. Magazine cartoons, of course, were nothing new. They were a staple of *Judge* (1881–1936), *Puck* (1877–1918), *Life* (1883–1936), and *Ballyhoo* (1931–1939), as well as *The New Yorker* (first published in 1925). The difference was the content. In an introduction to *The Esquire Cartoon Album* Arnold Gingrich writes,

> *Esquire*'s cartoons, in its earliest days, were much more of a novelty, in relation to other cartoons, than they can ever hope to be again. . . . [They] represented as close an approach to audience participation as the cartoon could ever come. . . . The most memorable example of this "Wanna Make Something Out Of It?" school of comic art was undoubtedly the drawing of the Petty girl looking you straight in the eye . . . and captioned, "Oh, you would, would you?" Cartoons like this brought scads of letters asking us to explain the point. We had to answer that there wasn't any, except as made by the mind of the beholder. . . . Again, it's a question of comparative novelty. We were the first with this type of pictorial humor. But

we always considered it, like paprika, something to be
used sparingly and with discretion.[38]

Gingrich called this approach Whamsy and says it was used only
sparingly, but most people called it Sex and said it was spread out
all over the magazine. Here is Henry Pringle's assessment of the *Esquire* cartoons from his *Scribner's* article:

> Subtlety or even variety are not of the essence of *Es-
> quire*. Familiarity, its management knows, is no bar to en-
> joyment of a good drawing. Thus there are many which
> appear again and again. A typical issue would be barren
> indeed without—in exact type at least—a majority of the
> following:
>
> Two blondes in their underwear: "Yeah, he insulted you
> and then what else did he do?"
>
> Man with dog talking into telephone, "Sweetheart, I've
> walked him around the block three times, but he doesn't
> seem to realize."
>
> Nudist camp scene.
>
> South Sea Island scene.
>
> Backstage, chorus-girl dressing-room scene.
>
> Hillbilly sketch, usually with an outhouse motif.
>
> A Petty Girl elevator operator, her skirt extremely tight,
> with two old codgers gazing lasciviously at her from the
> rear. Caption: "No particular floor, just drive up and
> down."
>
> Dydee Doll theme. A little boy being led down a Pull-
> man car toward "Women" sign. Caption: "Men, too?"
>
> Shotgun wedding.
>
> Girl in underwear examining jewelry while stout old
> man in dinner coat looks on. She says, "Of course, our
> friendship is all that matters."

Harem scene. For instance, the Sultan, trotting upstairs with a book under is arm while the mournful concubines gaze after him. Caption: "This is the third week he's gone to bed with Anthony Adverse."

Rather nervous young man seated on lounge with very attractive young woman in negligee. He is reading a volume vaguely marked "Love." Caption (she is speaking): "My God—quit reading about it!"[39]

The cartoonists whose work appeared most often in *Esquire* in the thirties were Howard Baer, who drew big, beautiful women overwhelming skinny little men; Syd Hoff, who made fun of the working class by drawing big, rounded lugs and lugettes; Paul Webb, whose specialty was lazy hillbillies; Dorothy McKay, who could draw in a variety of styles, almost to order; and Beverly Shermund, who specialized in cartoons about dumb blondes. Both Dorothy McKay and Beverly Shermund, in keeping with *Esquire* policy, used initials and not their first names, so readers would not know the magazine had female contributors.

In October 1933, the first *Esquire* hit the stands. Or, more properly, it hit the men's stores. There were 105,000 oversized copies of the 116-page magazine printed on slick paper to be sold at the then-staggering cost of fifty cents each. On the cover was a hunting scene showing two men arriving at a cabin on a lake by seaplane. A total of 100,000 copies were shipped to haberdashers to be sold from their counters. Another 5,000 were given to newsdealers to put on the stands as a way of legitimatizing it and to distinguish it from just another catalogue from the Men's Wear Service Corporation. *Esquire* was an instant hit. Copies of the magazine were called back from men's stores and sent to newsstands. It was a sellout. Originally planned as a quarterly, the magazine went monthly with its second issue.[40] David Smart, the barber's son from Chicago, had worked his way from the tenements of the West Side to the penthouses of the North Side and made it appear effortless. And at age twenty-nine, Arnold Gingrich, the woodcarver's boy from Grand Rapids, had hit the literary big time.

Esky: His Salad Days

he popular image of the era makes it seem impossible that a magazine like *Esquire* could be born in 1933 in the midst of the Great Depression, sell 100,000 copies of its first issue at a fifty-cent cover price, and make its principal reputation as an advisor to men on how to dress. But changes other than a flattened economy were going on in the United States, and these changes, often overlooked by popular histories, allowed *Esquire* to become a success.

Success is the right word to use in describing *Esquire*, because, bawdy cartoons, a growing literary reputation, and sexy pinups aside, that's what the magazine was about. To understand that, it's necessary to look back a decade before the magazine's inception. In the 1920s, urban population in the United States as a whole was greater than rural for the first time in the nation's history. And in that decade, the total population of the nation's cities grew by 14 million people. The twenties was also the decade when the values of persuasion (primarily advertising) and salesmanship and consumption began to replace those of hard work and thrift. Although the era of mass consumption had begun, it didn't take as many workers to produce products. As Warren Susman points out,

> While millions still labored to produce goods, fewer workers were needed to produce as much, and more and more people found themselves as professionals or in clerical or service trades. More found themselves on salary with all the assurances and possibilities for planning a life that meant. In the new world of abundance-leisure-consumer-pleasure orientation, more attention could be paid to gratification of personal needs of all kinds; and in fact, as it soon became clear, the new service industry of advertis-

ing would make every effort to stimulate those needs and awaken those desires in an effort to use them in creating a market for a whole new set of products. Strict codes of sexual morality would yield to what has been called a Freudian ethic.[1]

This world of the 1920s was new to everyone, but particularly to the many young men and women who moved from the farm to the city. How were they to behave? Could they conceal their ignorance of city ways? Was there a way they could become educated quickly and seem to be wise enough to carry on a conversation at a sophisticated cocktail party? These questions were pressing enough to create a whole new industry based on self-help and the popularization of high culture. In 1922, DeWitt Wallace started *The Reader's Digest*, which would let the otherwise uninformed read selections from a number of current periodicals. Three years later, the Book-of-the-Month Club was inaugurated so people would know which books to read. The books could be shipped to subscribers' homes to spare them the embarrassment of fumbling over volumes in a bookstore. History was popularized in the 1920s by H. G. Wells's *Outline of History*. With all this self-help, a man or woman from the sticks could at least take on enough of the trappings, vocabulary, and superficial sophistication of the city to belie his or her origins.

The 1920s and 1930s were also decades when personality became more important than character. Motion picture actors who became stars in the twenties—people like Clara Bow, the "It Girl" who won a fan magazine beauty contest and escaped Coney Island for good; Theda Bara, the mysterious Arabian femme fatale who was really from Cincinnati; Francis X. Bushman, who was a former sculptor's model from Norfolk, Virginia; and Clark Gable, who started his career as a rubber worker in Akron, Ohio—were noted for their perceived, screen-inspired personalities, not their offscreen characters. Babe Ruth, the baseball player, endeared himself to fans even though he was a gambling, heavy-drinking brothel patron. In 1925, Bruce Barton, a Tennessee preacher's son who became one of the nation's top advertising executives, described Christ's personality rather than his character in *The Man Nobody Knows*. Christ, Barton said in this book, was the most popular dinner guest in Jerusalem. In 1920, B. C.

Bean published *The Power of Personality*, in which he urged readers to "eliminate the little personal whims, habits, traits that make
people dislike you. Try in every way to have a ready command of the
niceties, the manners, the way of speech, etc. which make people
think, 'he's a mighty likable fellow.'"[2] In 1899 Orison Swett Marden
published *Character: The Greatest Thing in the World*. By 1921 he
had written another book, *Masterful Personality*. In his second book,
Marden emphasized manners, proper clothes, good conversation (to
know *what* to say and *how* to say it).

Words most frequently used to reflect character for men include
*citizenship, duty, democracy, work, building, golden deeds, outdoor
life, conquest, honor, reputation, morals, manners, integrity*, and
manhood. Adjectives used to express personality, on the other hand,
are *fascinating, stunning, attractive, magnetic, glowing, masterful,
creative, dominant*, and *forceful*.[3] By the 1930s, it was personality
that counted most. Dale Carnegie's book, *How to Win Friends and
Influence People*, became a bestseller in 1935, two years after the first
publication of *Esquire*.

It was this desire for self-help, this desire to fit in, develop a good
personality, and be able to advance in business, the whole rising tide
of expectations and aspirations, that *Esquire* exploited in a promotional advertisement in its October 1934 issue. Under a headline reading "Scram! said the Duchess . . . Until I Learned This Sure, Easy
Way to Fascinate Her . . . " appears the copy:

> All my life I had wanted to make a duchess . . . notice
> me. At last my opportunity had come. Was I in a dither!
> But somehow I couldn't get into Her Grace's graces. I
> couldn't even get into her lap! "Scram-mez-vous" she
> would say, in her charmingly modulated accent, whenever
> I tried to whisper a sweet nothing in her ear. (If you *think*
> it was nothing, you're crazy—but let's get on here.)
> Then one day my best friend told me! It was because I
> was a mug. Hadn't been anywhere. Hadn't seen anything.
> Didn't know anything. Did I say he was a friend? YES—
> because then he told me how to know everything a young
> man-about-town should know.
> Acting on his advice I rushed out and bought a copy

of *Esquire*. Even after reading that first copy, I noticed an amazing improvement. I could converse easily on modern arts and letters. I could tell the difference between a Chateau Lafitte 1926 and a Red Ink 1932. I knew how to distinguish Savile Row tailoring from Sears-Roebuck. I even knew a couple of head waiters.

From that day on, the duchess' manner toward me changed. I can truthfully say that had it not been for *Esquire* I would still be the simple hill-billy that my wife, the ex-duchess, first knew. You, too, can be a brilliant wit and beau this easy way. You never before bought so much delightful entertainment for so little. At all the BETTER newsstands.[4]

Even though the new idea of personality had supplanted the puritan notion of character, another piece of American mythology—pulling yourself up by your bootstraps—persevered. The reason for developing a personality was to get ahead, become a go-getter in the tradition of Horatio Alger's novels. Impoverished young men still believed they could struggle against poverty and gain wealth and fame. But the *Esquire* version of the myth allowed a little temptation from high living every once in a while. In fact, the temptations themselves seemed to offer another way of rising to the top.

The high living was often overshadowed by the magazine's role as a manual for survival in the new urban world. Before *Esquire*, when little was being written about men's fashion, it was not unusual to consult men's store employees to find out the correct way to dress and solve other masculine dilemmas. In Theodore Dreiser's *An American Tragedy*, for example, Clyde Griffiths consults with Orrin Short, "the young man conducting the one small 'gent's' furnishing store in Lycurgus in upper New York state which catered more or less exclusively to the rich youths of the city—a youth of about his own years and proclivities, as Clyde had guessed, who ever since he had been here had been useful to him in the matter of tips as to dress and style in general."[5] Clyde Griffiths had gotten a girl in trouble and was hoping Short, as a sophisticated masculine advisor, could direct him to the right kind of doctor. The Clyde Griffiths of America wouldn't have to rely on Orrin Short for sophisticated advice anymore. They could subscribe to *Esquire* instead, although the magazine, like Short, didn't supply the names of abortionists.

Even though the country was in the midst of the Depression, *Esquire* barely mentioned economic hard times in its first issue in December 1933. Instead, Gingrich chose to emphasize the optimism that came from Franklin Roosevelt's inauguration ten months earlier. On the opening page of the first issue he wrote:

> The New Deal has given leisure a new economic significance, and the five-day week has become not merely every man's right but virtually every man's duty.
>
> More time to read, more time to indulge in hobbies, to play, to get out of town—more time, in short, to think of Living as an art, as well as a business.
>
> Men have had leisure thrust upon them. Now they've got it, they must spend it somehow. Many of them—perhaps even the majority—haven't the faintest idea how to go about it.
>
> What more opportune occasion for the appearance of a new magazine—a new kind of magazine—one that will answer the question of What to do? What to eat, what to drink, what to wear, how to play, what to read—in short a magazine dedicated to the improvement of the new leisure.
>
> That magazine is *Esquire*. It is, as the name implies, a magazine for men. To analyze its name more closely, *Esquire* means, in the encyclopedia and dictionary sense, that class just below knighthood—the cream of that great middle class between nobility and the peasantry. In a market sense, however, *Esquire* means simply Mister—the man of the middle class. Once it was the fashion to call him Babbitt, and to think of him as a wheelhorse with no interests outside of business. That's very outmoded thinking, however. For today, he represents the New Leisure Class.
>
> This, then, is the story of the new magazine, *Esquire*, and of the new market that it opens up—a market that has been overlooked by editors and space buyers alike.[6]

According to the *Author Index to Esquire* by Herman Baron, only eight women were listed as contributors to the magazine in the thirties. The identity of female contributors was made by checking given names. Of course, there were those contributors who only used initials, which could be a cover for a woman. "H. Richards" was Helene Richards, an editorial assistant, and "C. McBride" was, in reality, Catherine McBride, the magazine's copy editor. There is also the possibility of pseudonyms. Mrs. Roy T. McCoy of Louisville, Kentucky, for example, wrote for *Esquire* in the forties under the name Gavin Gorman. The magazine was not particularly supportive of women in other ways, either. A random sample of eleven short stories published in the magazine in the 1930s shows that six of them have no female characters. Of the other five, women are only sex objects in four of them. It was not any better in nonfiction, with the worst example being "Women Are Like Gongs," by Bruce Henry, in the December 1937 issue. Henry suggests that both should be beaten regularly. Under a headline that read, "You should warn your wife when she's in for a beating, but don't go softie and allow her to coax you out of it," Henry wrote, "[Wife beating] is the regular, dispassionate, day-to-day lickings which produce results. . . . It is simply putting into place an age-old and very natural domestic custom."[7]

If sex was what sold the magazine to the male masses (by its second issue it had a circulation of 400,000 and by the spring of 1938 *Esquire* sold more than 750,000 copies), its dedication to men's fashion was what gave it appeal to advertisers. More than ten pages of each issue were devoted to what the well-dressed man should wear, usually full-page, full-color drawings giving explicit details of what a man should look like if he expected to get ahead. "Note that the width of the coat's collar and lapels is the same and that the coat itself is somewhat shorter than the topcoats have been in the previous season," read the copy under one picture. "Be sure that the trousers, even on a tweed suit, be pleated," said another. *Esquire*'s reputation as the arbiter of style for men was so pervasive that a spoof of the magazine (it was called *Squire*) furnished the plot line for the 1936 Fred Astaire/Ginger Rogers movie *Swing Time*. And, it seems, *Esquire* was always willing to help the poor clods who couldn't get dressed without it. At the bottom of each fashion page appeared the sentence, "For answers to all dress queries, send stamped, self-addressed envelope to Esquire Fashion Staff, 40 E. 34th, N.Y."

It may not have been *Esquire*'s goal to re-dress the white American man in sartorial splendor, but a quick look through the magazine makes it apparent that clothes not only make the man, they make up the bulk of *Esquire*'s advertising. Eighteen pages of the October 1934 issue are clothing ads. Twelve pages are devoted to ads for whiskeys and wines (Prohibition was repealed the month the magazine was first published). And, unlike the magazine itself, sex appeal is not used to sell clothes or whiskey. Instead, advertisers emphasize self-help and moving up the ladder of success. An ad for Finchley Tuxedos emphasizes "absolute correctness"; one for Manhattan shirts pushes "distinctive good taste"; Arrow shirts are claimed to be "for the man who wears the new styles first—who 'dictates' the clothes that other men follow"; Stetson Shoes tells readers, "Clothes may not make the man, but they can help send him through college— and life—creditably"; F. R. Tripler & Co. offers "distinctive correctness"; Covert Hats advertises "the new and correct color." *Correct* seems to be the watchword in these advertisements. And for the newly urbanized man who fears his small-town roots will show, being correct means fitting in to his new world. The ads themselves, unlike those that followed decades later, were designed to encourage men to buy their products to get ahead, not to get a girl.

There are no women pictured in the ads in the 1930s. Nor do they appear in the 1940s or the 1950s. Men's clothes were sold by male models. A change in advertising began to appear in the late 1960s when women as sex objects began to show up in ads for Curlee suits. By the March 1971 issue of *Esquire*, fully half of the clothing advertisements have women looking at the male model appreciatively. In the 1930s, clothes were sold as a necessary accoutrement on the road to success; by the 1970s, they were a lure on the road to successful sex. And unlike ads in the thirties, the later ads don't emphasize correctness, but sex appeal. "The most attractive men I know wear Japanese woolens," says a lovely women in an ad for the Japan Woolens Information Council; an ad for Jantzen features an attractive, miniskirted blonde hanging on the shoulders of the model wearing Jantzen clothes; a red-haired woman sits at the opposite end of a sofa from a man wearing a Gant shirt, her eyes shyly averted; a brunette stares with distinct interest at the man wearing Johnston and Murphy shoes; a man wearing Forge Ltd. trousers strokes the shoulder of an acquiescent blonde in a knit dress as the ad copy shouts, "He uses the same line on everyone." *Esquire* may have been a sexy magazine in the thirties, but sex was not used to sell products.

If women were not used as objects in *Esquire* advertising in the thirties and did not appear as wives or artists, how were they treated? For a magazine that encouraged wife beating and portrayed women as airheads, exactly as one would imagine. It was, in short, a sexist publication. As Henry Pringle said in *Scribner's* in 1938,

> It [*Esquire*] dares to deny that no American husband could possibly be betrayed by his wife, a theory which is part of the American credo. It dares, even, to offer the idea that the male may be less potent than the female. So the *Esquire* artists are encouraged to do timid men in the grip of dominating ladies. Among the most famous articles of the past three years was that by Helen Norden, anonymously published, called "Latins Are Lousy Lovers." This nearly caused Cuba to declare war on the United States and did result in the banning of the magazine in that jewel of the Caribbean. "She's no longer faithful if—" was the title of a series beginning early in 1936. It listed several hundred ways to detect wifely infidelity and it ran for five or six months.[8]

A check of the *Esquire* cartoons for the decade shows that women are sometimes drawn belittling men, receiving breakfast in bed from their husbands, being jilted, and facing sexual harassment from their bosses. But most of the time they are portrayed as being showgirls or ignorant bimbos, having ridiculous female quirks (betting, for example, at a racetrack window marked $1.98 instead of $2), and using their sexual allure for monetary gain. The women in the cartoons are usually shapely and as close to naked as possible. *Esquire* was no friend to women.

David Smart always said in interviews that *Esquire* was a magazine without an editorial policy. That wasn't true. Its policy, although never explicitly stated, was "The advertiser is always right." For example in October 1933 Gingrich wrote an apology for a story, "How Banks Betray the Public," which had appeared in the August issue. "*Esquire* regrets and regards as unfair the too general nature of the title," he wrote. "If we permitted Mr. Kelly [the writer of the banking article] to indulge in 'sinister insinuation' as to the probity of all bankers, then that was a foul by our own rules and we apologize."[9] Seven years later, the policy had not changed. In April 1941 *Esquire* apologized again, this time for running an article called "Go Get a Guitar," which said a guitar was better accompaniment for group singing than a piano. In a full-page editorial, Gingrich wrote, "We lost all our piano ads, like so many clay pigeons. . . . We can and do beg the pardon of the piano makers, severally and collectively, but we have no kick coming as we kiss the ads goodbye. We earned the rap we're taking."[10]

The magazine began as a quarterly with nine employees; it went monthly in its second issue, and by 1937 there were 275 people working full-time for *Esquire* in Chicago and New York. Included in the staff were 28 advertising salesmen, 16 artists drawing fashion and promotional layouts, 10 editors working under Gingrich, and 55 employees in the circulation and promotion department. *Esquire*'s printing (including typesetting, plates, paper, press work, and binding) cost 42 cents a copy in 1936, or $3,000,000 a year. But profits from newsstand sales, subscribers, and advertisers (gross advertising revenues for 1937 were estimated at $3,500,000; ads cost $2,800 a page and $5,900 for the back cover) allowed the magazine to turn a profit of $1.5 million a year. One way the magazine's profits stayed high was the low cost of its editorial product. The magazine rarely paid more than $200 for a story or $50 for a cartoon. *The New Yorker*, by comparison, paid $250 for a full-page cartoon, and *The Saturday Evening Post* paid $1,500 for a story by a top-name writer. Total editorial cost for *Esquire* was about $150,000 a year.[11]

The magazine attracted so many subscribers that the circulation department had to work its employees around the clock in eight-hour shifts. The work was so grueling, Gingrich remembers, that at three in the morning five women were sent home in cabs, weeping from overwork.[12] By the end of 1937, 10 million copies of *Esquire* had been sold. The $1.5 million in profit pouring into *Esquire*'s coffers each year meant a dramatic change for Gingrich and Smart. Their lives had been comfortable enough in the days of *Apparel Arts*, but now they were genuinely rich. So was Weintraub, but he was becoming more distant than ever from *Esquire*. As early as 1930, three years before *Esquire*, Smart had muscled Weintraub out of 5 percent of his stock in the corporation. Smart also agreed to get rid of 5 percent of his stock, and the 10 percent both men gave up went to Gingrich and Alfred Smart, who would have 5 percent each. That meant that in any corporate matters Weintraub, with his 45 percent of the stock, could expect no more than a standoff.

Gingrich left his Evanston apartment and moved into the city to a North State Parkway townhouse that cost him $42,000 cash and required six servants to run. The editor didn't have enough money to pay for the house, let alone keep up the servants, so Smart gave it to him. "Gingrich, this house is too good for you," Theodore Dreiser told him on his only visit to the mansion.[13] Smart was more flamboyant. He drove a black Duesenberg (Gingrich continued to drive a Ford) and moved into a bachelor apartment in the Drake Towers, across from the *Esquire*'s offices, where he slept in a circular bed. His office in the penthouse of the Palmolive Building on Michigan Avenue had chartreuse leather divans and featured pigskin-covered walls.

For all the trappings of wealth, working for *Esquire* could be an excruciating experience, particularly for Gingrich. Although he carried the title of editor, Smart never let him forget that it was the publisher who called the shots. On fishing trips to Florida, Smart would sometimes call back to Chicago and demand that the entire magazine be changed to include a manuscript he'd read or some new drawing he'd seen on the way to his vacation. Gingrich, and the whole *Esquire* staff, also had to endure Smart's two or three migraine headaches each week. "In the grips of a headache, he sometimes looks older than God," Gingrich told a reporter for *Time*.[14] Smart also suffered from hypochondria. He wouldn't touch a doorknob without first wiping it off with a handkerchief, and he constantly took medicine for ailments both real and imagined.[15]

One staff member who watched all of this was Meyer Levin (1905–1981), the Chicago author, who had already written four novels—*Reporter* (1929), *Frankie and Johnny* (1930), *Yehuda* (1931), and *The New Bridge* (1933)—when he came to work as assistant editor

of *Esquire* in 1934. Levin stayed with the magazine through 1938.
His job was helping Gingrich choose from the thousand manuscripts
a week that came into the office. He also was the movie reviewer, and
on weekends he slipped away to a shack at a nudist colony where he
wrote his novels.[16] The pressure of editing so many manuscripts
showed up in *Esquire*'s pages in 1935 when the magazine hailed Alvin
B. Harmon of Palisade, New Jersey, as its discovery of the month
for his short story "The Perlu." There was only one thing wrong.
"The Perlu" was really a plagiarized version of "The Damned Thing,"
a short story by Ambrose Bierce. It happened again in May 1937,
when *Esquire* published "The Tale of Three Cities" by Jed Kiley. The
story, it seems, had been published before—in the March 1932 edition of *College Humor* magazine as "The Eternal Triangle" by
Lichty.[17]

In his autobiography, *In Search* (1950), Levin described what it
was like to work at *Esquire*. He calls *Esquire* by the title *Paradise*,
and refers to Smart as Melvin Morris and Gingrich as Winters. Levin
uses pseudonyms, he says, because "in discussing matters of public
principle which were to arise between myself and the publisher, I do
not wish to seem to be motivated to call attention to actual persons
or institutions."[18]

Levin admired Smart, he said, and felt a kinship with him because
both were Jewish and both had been raised on Chicago's West Side.
He called him a "nerve-eaten idea man" who drove a hard bargain
but was open to new ideas. While at *Esquire* Levin developed the idea
of a handwritten rejection slip, which was used by the magazine for
decades. Smart, he writes, felt a sense of rivalry with *Time* that made
him grow bitter. *Esquire*, Levin says, had become known in the publishing world as a Jewish magazine, and *Time* was the epitome of non-
Jewishness. In 1939, on advice from advertising agencies on Madison
Avenue in New York, Smart decided to eliminate all Jewish bylines
from *Esquire*. That, of course, included Levin. "I've had my lesson,
and if I have to crawl on my knees to those people from here to New
York to save my business, I'm going to do it," Levin quoted Smart
as saying.[19]

In response, Levin decided to unionize *Esquire* that same year.
Gingrich was agreeable, although as management he couldn't join
the union, and Smart thought a union for upper editorial help would

be all right. But what Levin and his fifteen fellow employees were seeking, through the Book and Magazine Guild, was an organization that covered all employees—a shop and not a craft union. Levin remembers Smart countering the union idea by saying no fifteen-dollar-a-week typist was going to tell him how to run his business. One week, seven of the fifteen members of the potential union were fired. The next week, most of the others were dismissed. Levin took the matter before a labor board hearing and was advised that *Esquire* was antiunion, that a chance of winning was small, and that there was pressure from Washington to hush things up. The handful of union members remaining decided not to fight. Levin continued to write his film reviews but, after a few shouting matches with Smart over the telephone, quit working as an editor. His last review appeared under the byline "Patterson Murphy." Levin wrote, "I could only reflect on the curious self-hatred of the Jew, inventing such a joke."[20]

Also on staff as a cultural critic was Gilbert Seldes (1893–1970), the former editor (1920–1923) of *The Dial*; he wrote a monthly column, "The Lively Arts," for *Esquire*. Seldes was an ideal critic for *Esquire*, because in his earlier books, *The Seven Lively Arts* (1924) and *The Movies and the Talkies* (1929), he wrote about comic strips, movies, popular songs, and vaudeville. A critic with those interests was ideal for a magazine that was melding the highbrow and lowbrow. Novelists and critics hardly seem like ideal occupants of the offices of a fashion magazine, but William Weintraub told *The Literary Digest* there was no conflict. "They may come in here to work looking like Greenwich Village poets. But after a couple of months—well, even the artists wear clothes by Hart Schaffner and Marx."[21]

In 1935 Alfred A. Knopf published Gingrich's autobiographical novel, *Cast Down the Laurel*. In a novel-within-a-novel, the book told the story of a music school in Grand Rapids, Michigan. Peter Monro Jack, writing in *The New York Times*, called Gingrich's protagonist a "man of straw" and his minor characters "categories." But the review was not all bad. "Mr. Gingrich's technique does not live up to his conception, but there is enough interest in his first novel to hope for an extension . . . of the Midwest autobiographical realism that he knows so well."[22] The book was promoted with posters and an extensive advertising campaign, but it never made the bestseller list.

Most of the interest in *Cast Down the Laurel* was because Gingrich was editor of *Esquire*. It was Gingrich's only novel.

Esquire hit its circulation peak for the thirties in January 1938, with 728,000 copies sold.[23] Of that total, 48 percent of the circulation was in cities with populations of more than 100,000, and only 8.38 percent in towns of less than 2,500.[24] *Esquire* even spawned an imitator, *For Men*, a pocket magazine filled with articles and cartoons in the *Esquire* style published by Fawcett Publications. The magazine's demographics in the 1930s showed that 10 percent of its readers earned more than $5,000 a year and that 80 percent made from $2,000 to $5,000 or more.[25] In an advertising brochure, the magazine said of its typical reader,

> He is a very shaky bet to endow any universities, or to leave monuments behind him in the shape of any such good and lasting works. He drinks too much. He drives too fast. And he swears on no provocation at all. As his pal we will stoutly maintain that his interest in sex is healthy, but we cannot deny it is lively. And he hasn't been to church since the last time he ushered at a wedding. And try as we may, we have yet to find a subject which he considers sacred. He's a sailor with his money—he sails for every new thing that comes into his ken and, more often than not, for no good reason. He's rather inclined to be vain and self indulgent. . . . There's an even chance that you would hesitate to accept him for some things. Quite possibly you would hesitate to take him into the bosom of your family, or even to propose him for membership in your club. But you couldn't possibly hesitate to accept his business because the Grade-A spender is the prime prospect.[26]

Although the booklet was describing *Esquire*'s typical reader in the 1930s, it sounds more like a collegiate escort for a flapper a decade before. Or, as Henry Pringle wrote, "He is a far cry from the devotee of the New Deal's New Leisure for whom, when it all began, the magazine was to be edited. . . . What he likes is the old leisure of 1929—and what he stands for is more mistresses and more champagne."[27]

Smart extended his realm in 1936 by moving some of *Esquire*'s most popular features into newspaper syndication. Called Esquire Features, Inc., the syndicate was run by Howard Denby, a former editor with the *Chicago News*. In addition to some of the less sexy *Esquire* cartoons and the magazine's fashion features, the syndicate represented *Chicago News* writer Howard Vincent O'Brien and his column, "All Things Considered"; Bob "Bazooka" Burns, a former vaudevillian and radio comedian who wrote rural humor; Hedda Hopper, a Hollywood columnist; Elsa Maxwell, a prominent hostess; and Constance Bennett, a movie star. The syndicate was short-lived—it was closed by 1940—but it showed that Smart was trying to move his business interests beyond the confines of the magazine's pages. His next project, reminiscent of his days as a sugar speculator, would get him in trouble.

In 1937, when *Esquire* was at the peak of its popularity, Smart went public and put the company on the American Stock Exchange. Just before he offered the stock, *Esquire* employees were allowed to buy it at $16 a share. When *Esquire* became a public corporation, the price of the 75,000 shares fell to $12 a share. Smart turned around and gave more stock (for a total of 153,000 shares) to employees, and that reduced the price to $8 a share.[28] The Brothers Smart made a profit on the stock sale of $1,075,000. They also declared false profits of $807,000 by listing circulation and promotion expenses as an asset instead of a liability. Had they not done that, profits would have been $205,000 less. For artificially manipulating the price of the stock, Smart, his brother Alfred, and ten others were indicted in 1938 for conspiracy to violate the Securities and Exchange Act of 1934. The law says the price of stock must remain stable during a sales period. At the time of the indictment, the price of *Esquire* stock was less than $3 a share.[29] In September of 1941, the Smart brothers entered a plea of *nolo contendre*, "accepting judgment without admitting guilt." They were fined $10,000 each and sentenced to two years in prison. Prison sentences were suspended on payment of the fines. Newspapers and magazines gave full coverage to Smart's problems. *Time* called it the "Saga of Smart," and *Business Week* wrote about the "SEC and *Esquire*."

By June of 1938, *Esquire*'s circulation dropped to 453,000.[30] It appeared that the magazine's boom was over. By the beginning of

1939, however, circulation was back up—but only to 525,000. Much of the additional circulation (80,000) came from the subscription list from *Scribner's* that Smart bought in 1939, a year after that magazine suspended publication.[31] That same year Smart also enlarged the size of the Petty Girl, making her a foldout instead of a one-page cartoon, but that didn't provide the boost the magazine needed. Part of the reason for the circulation drop was a recession. Part of it may have been that the magazine's novelty had worn off. A full 40 percent of the magazine's sales were on newsstands as late as 1940, indicating that it was a magazine bought occasionally on impulse and not delivered regularly at home by mail.[32]

Of course, *Esquire* didn't die at the end of the decade, but it was world events, and more pinups, that made it prosper. "It was a fabulous success for a while, but they damn near went broke," remembers Jerry Jontry. "Actually Abe Blinder [former circulation director and chairman of the board of *Esquire*] said that if it hadn't been for the war [World War II] they would have gone broke. The war saved them because it guaranteed them circulation to the boys abroad."[33] But there was more going on in the penthouse offices of *Esquire* than just the woes of the company's parent magazine. Smart had started three other publishing ventures, *Ken, Coronet,* and *Verve,* and the fortunes of these three magazines helped to weaken the Smart empire so much that only a world war could save it.

5 Other Parts of the Empire

y the late 1930s, at the height of *Esquire*'s success, David Smart felt confident enough to brag to a reporter from *Time*, "Why didn't somebody tell me about this publishing game before? It's a cinch."[1] In the next few years, Smart set out to prove his point by establishing three new magazines—*Coronet, Verve*, and *Ken*. It was Smart's effort at building an empire to compete with the New York giants like Henry Luce's Time, Inc., but it was an effort built on sand. Most of the new Smart magazines lasted for only a few years and left Esquire, Inc., gasping for breath. Yet during those years, *Esquire* was the corporate name for some of the strangest publications published in America. First, there was *Coronet*.

In the United States, collecting great art has always been associated with the upper classes. In turn-of-the-century Europe, royalty commissioned paintings. In America, Gilded Age millionaires like William Randolph Hearst and Andrew Mellon raided European castles when the empires crumbled and brought the treasures across the Atlantic. To have a collection of paintings confirmed you as a kind of American royalty. The idea of the collector as royalty continued into the 1920s when John Ringling, one of the owners of the Ringling Brothers and Barnum & Bailey Circus, began collecting art by Rubens, Titian, Rembrandt, and other European masters.[2] And then a decade after Ringling, there was David Smart. Starting in 1932 Smart began collecting paintings by Renoir, Chagall, Soutine, Marquet, Vlaminck, Terechkovich, Utrillo, Pascin, and Cassatt. But there was a difference in these collectors. Mellon and Ringling made their art available to the public in museums; Smart started a magazine that reproduced great art and charged a quarter for it. In 1936, when *Esquire* was making so much money it needed a tax write-off, Smart decided to put out an art magazine. It was titled *Coronet*, after the novel of the same name by Manual Komroff, and it would, as Arnold Gingrich wrote, "give the public what it ought to like, whether it liked it or not."[3]

Actually, Smart's new magazine was not alone in its attempt to bring "high art" to the masses. Network radio in the late 1930s and early 1940s had its share of classical music—the Metropolitan Opera, hosted by Deems Taylor, a composer and conductor, and sponsored by Texaco; the NBC Symphony Orchestra, conducted by Arturo Toscanini and sponsored by General Motors; the New York Philharmonic on CBS, sponsored by United States Rubber; and the Boston Symphony, sponsored by Allis Chalmers. Orson Welles broadcast radio versions of the classics on the Mercury Theater of the Air; Archibald MacLeish, Stephen Vincent Benét, and Edna St. Vincent Millay wrote poetic drama for radio. But there was no more altruism involved in these radio productions than there was in Smart's effort to get a tax break. Networks were under siege from opponents of commercial broadcasting and scheduled these cultural programs during time periods they couldn't sell. They were often pitted, as a sort of cultural loss-leader, against more popular and profitable programs like *Fibber McGee and Molly* or *Edgar Bergen and Charlie McCarthy*. With these programs, broadcasting executives could fend off their critics by pointing to the cultural activities they were broadcasting. And the sponsors of these highbrow shows could deduct the money spent on them as a tax loss.[4]

Smart decided the new magazine would exist on circulation revenue alone. It would be a pocket-size magazine, like *The Reader's Digest*, which at that time didn't take advertising either. Gingrich gave *Coronet* its slogan, "Infinite riches in a little room," which he took from Christopher Marlowe. Like all Smart magazines, it was produced on the cheap. Gingrich was sent to museums and collectors to arrange for photographs of small items, like Japanese netsuke figures, Persian miniatures, or eighteenth-century dance favors, that would look good as full-page illustrations in a digest-size magazine. Of course, the owners were not paid for the right to use the objects. The museums, and possibly private owners as well, agreed to have their collection in *Coronet* for either ego or publicity. Early issues of the magazine also included reproductions of paintings by Raphael and Rembrandt. But in his race to profit from high culture, Smart had not forgotten the lesson he learned from *Esquire*: sex sells. Each issue carried a section called "Photographer's Gallery": it featured black-and-white contemporary photos of nude women.

Smart said his goal was to show that "beauty was still a very potent market" and to see that *Coronet* was recognized as "the most beautiful of magazines."[5] *Coronet* was announced with a two-page advertisement in *The Saturday Evening Post*. The first issue went on sale in November 1936 with a press run of 250,000 copies. Newsstands across the country were sold out in forty-eight hours. The magazine continued throughout the late 1930s, giving readers a heavy dose of modern and classical paintings, photographs, fiction, and poetry. Smart hired Deems Taylor, the voice of the radio broadcasts of the Metropolitan Opera, to promote *Coronet* by conducting symphony concerts sponsored by *Coronet*. But the magazine never caught on. Even the nude photographs couldn't keep sales up, and by 1940, circulation dropped to 87,000. The magazine was failing fast until Oscar Dystel took over as editor in 1940.

Dystel was born in New York City in 1912. He graduated from New York University and then received a master's degree from the Harvard School of Business, where his thesis was a comparison of controlled circulation and paid circulation in business magazines. In 1937 he went to work in the circulation department of *Sports Illustrated* (not the Luce publication, but an earlier magazine of the same name, edited by Grantland Rice) and *The American Golfer*. Even though those magazines failed, Dystel was hired by Alfred Smart to work in *Esquire*'s circulation and promotion department. At the time, in 1938, *Esquire*'s circulation was slipping for the first time, and the Smarts hoped Dystel could shore it up. A couple of years after he moved to Chicago, Dystel began working out changes for *Coronet*, which was in the midst of its circulation nosedive. He wrote a report on a change in *Coronet*'s focus as if it were a thesis, and gave it to Abe Blinder, the circulation director, who showed it to David Smart. A day later, Smart came into Dystel's office and appointed the promotions expert editor of *Coronet*. "Me, an editor," Dystel remembers. "And I didn't know a writer from a hole in the wall."[6]

What Dystel said in his proposal was that *Coronet* could no longer be an arts magazine if it were to succeed. He wanted to drop the highbrow features and make the magazine more accessible to the middle classes. That meant making it more like *The Reader's Digest* and its scores of imitators, including *Science Digest, Catholic Digest, Negro Digest, Children's Digest,* and *Everybody's Digest.* The digest became a popular form in American publishing after the success of *The Reader's Digest,* which was founded in 1922 by DeWitt Wallace, the son of a St. Paul Presbyterian minister. The *Digest* formula called for applicability—the reader should feel the subject concerned him; lasting interest—an article should be worth reading years later; and constructiveness—the writing should feature optimism and good works. By 1940, *The Reader's Digest,* which carried no advertising, had a circulation of four million. Dystel's even more immediate model for the new *Coronet* was *American Weekly,* the Hearst Sunday supplement, which had a circulation of almost ten million and was the most widely read magazine in the world.[7] *American Weekly's* content was mostly inspirational. The formula for the typical new *Coronet* story might be, as Gingrich said, "You, too, can succeed though one-legged and blind."[8] Dystel combined the articles with photo essays that were inspired by Henry Luce's newsreel, *The March of Time.* The cover of the magazine changed from paintings like Ghirlandaio's portrait of a lady of the Sassetti family to photographs of models and Hollywood starlets.

But *Coronet's* new editor had to deal with the same problem Gingrich faced on *Esquire*—a meager editorial budget. Dystel wanted to continue good illustration—not the high art pictures of *Coronet's* first incarnation, but illustrations that would appeal to middlebrow readers. He wanted to hire painters like Norman Rockwell, but there was no money. So he came up with a scheme. On trips to New York, Dystel would rent a car and drive to New England, where, he had discovered, most of the top magazine illustrators lived. The editor would drop in on the artists unannounced and look around their studio for a painting that hadn't sold. Dystel identified himself as a representative of the Curtis Company (the publishers of *The Saturday Evening Post*), which was not a complete lie since Curtis distributed *Esquire* and *Coronet,* and asked if he could take a picture of the painting and reproduce it. Usually, the artists said yes. Back in Chicago, a writer would be hired to write an essay about the painting for *Coronet.* The illustrators never got a dime.[9] But, of course, they got good publicity that might have meant more sales of other work.

Dystel also raised *Coronet*'s circulation with promotional schemes. He began a series on genealogy that featured the origins of a different American family name each month. The first name in the series was Johnson, because, Dystel says, there were more Johnsons in the phone book than any other name. After the story was scheduled, the *Coronet* staff sent out postcards to all the Johnsons in the country, telling them there would be an article of special interest to anyone named Johnson in the next issue. The series continued for years.

Dystel phased out the nude studies, but continued for a while to include pictures of starlets including, in the late 1940s, the first publication of the nude picture of Marilyn Monroe that would become a calendar favorite and, in 1953, the first *Playboy* Playmate. According to Dystel, the cheesecake pictures were bundled in the center of the magazine so a male reader could tear out those pages and bring home a magazine that was otherwise suitable for the family. Dystel made his changes slowly, a little in each issue, so he could hold on to old readers while attracting new ones. Circulation soared. It was estimated at five million during the boom years of World War II, but dropped to two million in 1947.

Editorial content of the Dystel *Coronet* was never memorable. Magazine historian Roland Wolseley writes that the Dystel version of the magazine was "divested of its exclusiveness, originality, and artistic appeal."[10] Its literary content was on a par with its other pocket magazine competitors, *Your Life, Your Health,* and *Your Personality,* all published by Wilfred J. Funk, whose father had been a founder of *The Literary Digest.*[11]

Dystel left *Coronet* briefly in 1942 to work for the Office of Wartime Information, editing a propaganda magazine distributed by the American armed forces during World War II. He returned to *Coronet* in 1944 and stayed through 1948. Upon his return, he felt David Smart looking over his shoulder, and it made him uncomfortable. Even though he was editor and had turned the magazine around, Dystel was never allowed to see any of *Coronet*'s financial records. In 1941, however, *Time* reported that *Coronet* was "breathing down the neck" of *The Reader's Digest.*[12] By 1947, Dystel and Smart were arguing over whether the magazine should include advertising. Smart wanted it, but Dystel was determined to keep the magazine the way it was and raise the cover price. Smart ignored Dystel and announced advertising for the magazine.

In 1948, Dystel left *Coronet* to become managing editor of *Collier's*. Six years later he ended his career in magazines and became one of the founders of Bantam Books, one of the most successful of the mass-market paperback publishers. *Coronet* continued, with advertising, through the early 1960s. Under its new editors, Harris Shevelson and Lewis Gillenson, the magazine published less inspirational material and used more reader-participation content like puzzles and games. It also dropped editorial independence and tailored its content to the wants of advertisers.[13] The race for gigantic circulation that overtook the magazine industry in the late 1950s and early 1960s as a way to combat television killed *Coronet* the same way it choked *Collier's* and *The Saturday Evening Post. Coronet* and the other magazines that died in the circulation wars had lots of readers, but not enough advertisers to pay for the cost of producing the magazine.[14] In 1961, Esquire, Inc., negotiated with other publishers to buy *Coronet. The Reader's Digest* bought a $1,300,000 ten-color press the company had installed three years earlier and split the *Coronet* circulation list with the Curtis Publishing Company.

Three years later, Arnold Gingrich delivered the *Coronet* epitaph: "[*Coronet*] became that anomaly, the world's largest midget, or the world's smallest giant, neither of which is a title with great natural box office potentialities. In any event, it wound up in 1961 with insufficient riches in too little room. It lived to attend its twenty-fifth birthday party, reminding me of the League of Nations buildings in Geneva, which were finished just in time for World War II."[15]

David Smart got involved in another art magazine in 1937 when he was in Paris receiving acupuncture treatments for his migraine headaches. After visiting the acupuncturist, Smart stopped by the apartment of an expatriate friend, where he met Edouard Teriade, the editor of the French magazine *Minotaure*. Teriade's magazine had run out of money, and he had been thrown out of his office.[16]

Minotaure began publication in 1933 with Teriade as editor and Albert Skira as publisher. It soon became the unofficial magazine of the surrealists. René Magritte painted covers for the magazine. So did Man Ray, Salvador Dali, Max Ernst, and Pablo Picasso. Inside there were articles about Dogon funeral dances by Michel Leiris; reviews of Picasso's work by André Breton, one of the founders of surrealism; a long treatise by Jean Levy on *King Kong*, a favorite film of the surrealists; the development of Dali's "paranoia-criticism"; and articles about psychiatry by Jacques Lacan.[17] Other artists who contributed to the magazine included Jean Arp, Paul Delvaux, Paolo Giacometti, Joan Miró, Yves Tanguy, and Marcel Duchamp.[18]

Smart agreed to buy the magazine from Teriade and gave him a thousand dollars. This was the beginning of a colossal misunderstanding. Teriade was a Greek who spoke French but no English, and Smart was an American who didn't know a word of French. As it turned out, Smart only bought copies of ten issues of *Minotaure*, not the magazine itself, as he thought. Teriade couldn't have sold the magazine anyway; it was owned by Albert Skira, the man who had just fired him as editor. *Minotaure*, it seems, had not run out of money, Teriade had run out of a job. Skira had decided not to pay his editor any more and had thrown him out of the magazine's offices.

When Smart found out about the mix-up, he didn't care. He sent Gingrich to Paris to work out the arrangements for an international art magazine, a quarterly, to be priced at $2.50 a copy. Teriade no longer had *Minotaure*, but his contacts from his work as editor of that magazine were intact, and he was able to enlist Picasso, Matisse, and Chagall to work for the new magazine; he also secured the cooperation of a number of Paris art museums in making works available for reproduction. Gingrich named the new magazine *Verve*. Under Smart's ownership, it lasted only four issues. Smart gave the rights to the title back to Teriade and his mistress, Angele La Motte, who produced one more American edition, to be sold at the 1939 World's Fair, and then returned to France. After World War II the magazine continued, with special editions devoted to Matisse, Picasso, and Roualt. Despite his love for art, Smart had no luck in publishing magazines about it. Besides, when he had relinquished control of *Verve*, he had gotten interested in politics.

Smart may have started thinking about a political magazine after spending the night in the White House as Franklin Roosevelt's guest.[19] This may be where he sold the President's son, James, one hundred shares of *Esquire* stock.[20] According to Meyer Levin, who worked for both *Esquire* and *Ken*, the first sign that Smart was thinking politics was the change in cartoons posted on the walls of the publisher's office. Usually the pigskin walls were covered with "sexy babe" cartoons. But, in 1938, drawings by Gropper of *The New Masses* began showing up. Smart was also beginning to talk enthusiastically about writers for leftist magazines—George Seldes, John Spivak, Claude Cockburn. Levin remembers the conversation:

> Now take their *New Masses*. What was their circulation? Maybe twenty thousand tops. Those lefties had no idea how to promote a magazine. . . . Excitedly my boss began to expound—a magazine for the people! Big articles about medical care for all, about how unions and employers could cooperate, big exposes of the Silver Shirts, the Bund. . . . [Smart] had been touched by the Roosevelt magic. He was dreaming of a liberal magazine.[21]

By 1937, liberalism had become the dominant political ideology in the United States. A year before, Roosevelt had been elected to a second term, carrying all but two states. It was a stunning affirmation of the President's New Deal policies, which were more liberal than any prior governmental efforts this country had known. The National Labor Relations Act was passed by Congress in 1936, which prompted the formation of the Congress of Industrial Workers and made industry-wide unions possible.

And liberalism was not limited to practical politics. The theater was teeming with leftist ideas—Orson Welles produced and directed *Macbeth* with an all-black cast as part of the government-sponsored Federal Theater Project (1936); Clifford Odets was having enormous success with his pro-union play, *Waiting for Lefty* (1935); Marc Blitzstein wrote an opera, *The Cradle Will Rock*, about labor strife (1937); *Dead End* (1935), a play about life in New York tenements, ran for 687 performances on Broadway; *The Living Newspaper* series (1935–1937), written by Elmer Rice and other playwrights, brought current issues to the stage with a leftist point of view; the International Ladies' Garment Workers' Union produced a musical, *Pins and Needles* (1937), which ran for 1,108 performances on and off Broadway.

The same leftist ideas showed up in literature, particularly in the works of the proletarian writers. John Dos Passos espoused a leftist point of view in his trilogy, *USA* (1930–1936); Robert Cantwell wrote about a strike in a lumber mill in *The Land of Plenty* (1934); Josephine Herbst detailed the social frustrations of an American family in *The Executioner Waits* (1934); Jack Conroy chronicled picket lines and soup kitchens in *The Disinherited* (1933); Henry Roth described life in a Jewish ghetto in *Call It Sleep* (1934); and Richard Wright explained what it was like to be black in a white America in *Uncle Tom's Children* (1938).

Nor was leftist thought absent from the visual arts. The murals of Mexican artist Diego Rivera, who was a communist, were painted in public buildings in Detroit (1933), New York (1934), and San Francisco (1939). His artistry inspired the federal government's Public Works of Art mural project, which commissioned murals in post offices and other public buildings throughout the United States.

So Smart's idea of starting a liberal consumer magazine didn't seem like an ideological gamble. It seemed like a cinch.

Smart thought he and his new political magazine could save the American worker with journalism. On a boat trip to Paris in 1937, he told Jay Allen, a foreign correspondent for the *Chicago Tribune*, "This magazine will be the first big break the underdog in America has had."[22] Arnold Gingrich remembers Allen as being crucial to the founding of *Ken*:

> We [Smart and Gingrich] got the idea for [*Ken*] in the summer of 1937. We had fallen into the habit, every morning, of reading Jay Allen's dispatches from the Spanish Civil War in the *Chicago Tribune* when we were having our morning coffee. . . . we were both moved by the plight of the loyalists, outraged at the cynical deliberations of the so-called "non-interventionist" council meetings . . . and both completely convinced that the Germans and the Italians were using the war simply as a trial run for the war they were preparing in Europe. We used to feel like cheering every time Jay Allen called a spade a spade in his dispatches from Spain. . . . Inevitably he [Smart] began trying to figure out how we could get a whole magazine of "stuff like this Jay Allen writes."[23]

After Allen was fired by the *Chicago Tribune* a short time later, he met with Smart and Gingrich, and they agreed to work together to put out an insider's news magazine emphasizing problems in Europe.

Smart understood consumer magazines, but had no feeling for the difference between mass-market and opinion publications and probably had no notion of the complexity and range of political ideologies. Most opinion magazines want to spread the word; Smart wanted to make money doing it. The history of political magazines in the United States, particularly leftist political journals, is altogether different from the business of consumer publications, which Smart had mastered. Opinion magazines rely on donations from wealthy benefactors or contributions from a large number of people, not advertising, to keep them afloat.

Consider first the case of *The Nation*, which started publication in 1865. That publication was founded with $100,000 raised from forty wealthy stockholders who believed in Frederick Law Olmstead's idea of liberal journalism. Principal contributors were James Miller McKin of Philadelphia, George L. Stearns and Charles Eliot Norton of Boston, and Edwin Lawrence Godkin of New York.[24] In later years the magazine existed on the largesse of the Villard railroad fortune and the Kirstein department store money.[25] *The New Republic* was founded by Dorothy Whitney Straight, whose parents were William C. Straight and Flora P. Whitney of New York. Straight's father had been secretary of the navy under Cleveland and was a financier and traction magnate. Her mother was the daughter of Senator Henry B. Payne of Ohio, who was once treasurer of the Standard Oil Company. The magazine, which began publication in 1914, lived off the Straight money until 1953.[26] *The Masses*, a socialist/literary magazine that began publication in 1911, was initially financed by Rufus Weeks, a vice-president of the New York Life Insurance Company. He was only the first in a series of rich patrons for the magazine until it was killed by the federal government in 1917.[27] Max Ascoli, an Italian political scientist who was run out of Italy during the 1930s for his antifascist writing, started *The Reporter* in 1949 with money supplied by his wife, Marion Rosenwald, an heiress to the Sears, Roebuck fortune.[28] Even the New York leftist daily, *PM* (1940–1948), began with no advertising, promoting that as a virtue because, as one of its early staff members said, it probably wouldn't be able to get any anyway. After a shaky first three months of publication, *PM* stayed in existence only through the money of Marshall Field, the Chicago department store owner.[29]

So in 1937, when Smart began making plans to publish a leftist consumer magazine reporting on national and international affairs, with the money from the publication to come from advertising revenues, he was swimming upstream. Consider the other mass-market consumer magazines of the era that covered politics and it becomes even more apparent. *The Saturday Evening Post*, when revitalized by Curtis, was founded "on the proposition that a man's chief interest in life is the fight for livelihood—business." On the stage, in fiction, in articles, he thought, the business world was being misrepresented. Curtis reasoned that businessmen would welcome a magazine carrying authoritative articles and stories about business.[30] And *Time*, from its beginning, celebrated Republicanism and businessmen. In 1929 the magazine featured business tycoons on its cover sixteen times. The other Luce publication of the era, *Fortune*, first published in 1929, proclaimed the "generally accepted commonplace that America's greatest achievement has been business."[31] In fact, the power of advertisers (specifically their threat of financial retaliation), seems to be what killed the muckraking movement of the turn of the century.[32]

Smart thought he and his magazine were above threats from Madison Avenue. *Coronet* had no advertising and *Esquire* couldn't be touched. Although the creation of the new political magazine involved an ideological commitment—in discussing the magazine Smart talked of the old days when his family had been poor and his aunt was a friend of Eugene Debs—the publisher seemed to believe it made economic sense as well. "Even if I were merely doing *Ken* as a business proposition," he said, "it would be O.K. Here's this new reservoir—the labor movement, the A. F. of L., the C. I. O., the American Labor Party, the progressives in the West—ten to twenty million people who can read. We're going to try to tap this reservoir." In some ways, Smart's idea was not as outrageous for the times as it now seems. After all, Gene Autry recorded "The Death of Mother Jones." When asked about possible pressure from big business and advertisers, including the possibility they might attack *Esquire*, Smart opened a copy of *Esquire* and said, "Seventy per cent men's clothes, 20 per cent whiskey and soda; what is there to expose? We're invulnerable. They can't attack us."[33]

The magazine was named *Ken—The Insider's World* by Gingrich. It was the Scottish use of the word meaning "understanding," not a man's name, that Gingrich had in mind. In early August of 1937, Smart hosted a well-publicized dinner to announce the launching of *Ken*. Ernest Hemingway sat at the place of honor on Smart's left, and it was at least implied that he would have a prominent place with the forthcoming magazine. Within the week, Hemingway left for Europe.[34] Once back in Chicago, Smart received a letter from Jay Allen in Paris. *Ken,* he wrote, was to be a magazine for the coming people's front in America, was to take no sides in factional disputes of labor organizations and liberal-labor parties but was to represent a united front of all decent and intelligent liberal and progressive elements. After reading his letter, Smart cabled Allen, "thrilled by your letter."[35]

Initially, Smart gave Jay Allen thirty thousand dollars to hire a staff and prepare a dummy. Since the magazine was to be a cross between *Fortune* and *The Nation*, Allen and his staff prepared a twenty-thousand-word feature about fascist wars on democracy for the first time. Then Smart changed his mind. The Luce publication he wanted to imitate was *Time*. Why all this emphasis on imitating a Luce magazine? Meyer Levin believed it was because Smart saw a chance to "prove to the world that a Jew was no kike," and "to assert his wrath against a superior gentile world [where] he was a citizen, a human being who saw the linked injustices of our civilization." And although Levin says he believes Luce was not anti-Semitic, he was puzzled by "constant innuendos in that magazine. I know that . . . some sensitive Jewish readers were . . . apprehensive of *Time*." Levin remembers Smart saying, "Those New York operators would learn a thing or two! Within a year there would be only one big name in the magazine field; *David Smart!*"[36] Oscar Dystel put it more simply: "David seemed to admire WASPs." Dystel felt Smart was ambivalent about his Jewishness. "When I quit *Coronet* after working there ten years, David Smart asked me to reconsider. 'Talk it over with your priest,' he said. 'But David,' I answered, 'I'm Jewish.'"[37]

A new dummy that looked more like *Time* was prepared, and articles were shortened. Smart changed his mind again, and this time he fired Allen and most of his staff. The publisher told people he had spent thirty thousand dollars and had nothing to show for it.

That, he said, was why Allen was fired, not because of any political dispute but simply because he had frittered away the seed money and never done any work. Gingrich defended Smart's decision to fire Allen:

> That fall . . . Jay Allen came back [from Europe] with just about as much done, for his new magazine, as he had that first day in Chicago, before he took the thirty thousand dollars and the trip that was supposed to result in virtually a finished magazine. He still had a small dummy, made of folded-over sheets of hotel stationery, on which were scribbled one or two names and/or topics per page and nothing else. . . . Dave decided . . . that not another cent was going to be paid over to Jay Allen. He had had his turn at bat and struck out. "We gotta give this guy the bum's rush tomorrow," Dave said.[38]

But George Seldes, who later became the editor of *Ken,* believes that lack of work and nothing to show for Smart's expenditures was not the reason for Allen's dismissal:

> I have seen the dummies, layouts, stories, illustrations, and photographs which Allen prepared, all accurate and interesting pieces, superior to anything which has yet appeared in *Ken,* and yet I have heard Smart sneer about spending forty or fifty thousand dollars on the Allen regime "and not having a damn thing to show for it." I am now convinced that a desire to economize, not the style or the character of the magazine as worked out by Allen, caused the eventual separation of Smart and Allen.[39]

In both *Coronet* and *Esquire* Smart had held editorial expenses to the minimum, so there is no reason to quarrel with Seldes's assessment. And Meyer Levin agreed:

> *Time* and *Life* required a mammoth staff, correspondents on high salaries and expenses all over the world. Yet there was a way to get the best material, the inside stuff,

for practically nothing. Take the foreign correspondents—
every one of them had a story he was itching to tell but
which no publication dared print. For a nominal price,
without having to keep writers on the payroll or cover their
travelling expenses, one could obtain the best material. It
was a variation of the [*Esquire*] formula: there was good
material without a market that could be had cheaply.
Among those lefties were the cleverest cartoonists, the wit-
tiest writers, the sharpest reporters, all with material they
were aching to get before a mass public.[40]

After the Allen staff was fired, Smart and Gingrich approached
George Seldes, whose younger brother, Gilbert, wrote an arts column
for *Esquire* in the 1930s, about editing *Ken*. Seldes, born in 1890 in
New Jersey, worked as a reporter and foreign correspondent until
1927. After that he was best known for his exposés. His books included *You Can't Print That! The Truth Behind the News, 1918–
1929* (1929); *Can Those Things Be* (1931); *Sawdust Caesar* (1935),
a look at Italian fascism; *World Panorama* (1933), a study of the
post–World War I world; *The Vatican* (1934); *Iron, Blood and Profits*
(1934), about the ammunition industry; and *Freedom of the Press*
(1935). Seldes writes, "I was shown the supposedly final prospectus
which was to bear out the magazine's stated purpose—*Ken* will be
one step left of center . . . anti-war and anti-fascist." Two solid pages
boasted that the magazine would not be objective but biased—no-
bly biased in favor of the awakening liberal-labor movement in
America.[41]

Seldes was initially hired to edit the press section of *Ken*, which
was to cover about a third of the magazine, or thirty thousand words.
The section would include a "lie detector" to which members of the
American Newspaper Guild, the journalists' union, would contribute. Once each month (the magazine was to be published fortnightly)
there would be an investigation of the press in one of the country's
big cities. *Ken*'s motto was a modification of the one used by Charles
A. Dana, the editor of the New York *Sun*. Dana had said, "What the
good Lord lets happen, I am not ashamed to print." Gingrich changed
ashamed to *afraid*.[42] The press department never appeared in print.

Again, Gingrich acts as Smart's apologist:

When I saw George Seldes's dummy of what purported to be an entire issue, I thought he was joking. It was all done with scissors and a paste pot. There would be a pasted down block of copy (some news story or other) and beneath it, written with grease pencil in a bold hand, the words "This is a lie!" Then another pasted down block of copy, and again the interstitial interjection, though varying slightly, between every two blocks of pasted down copy, "This is a damnable lie" or "This is a foul lie" or "This is an outrageous lie." I couldn't believe it.[43]

Judging from Gingrich's comments, he and Smart didn't want an editor; they wanted a technician who could do layout and design the physical magazine. And yet they continued to hire writers. Then they fired the writers, ostensibly because they were not technicians.

As gossip columnists and trade magazines spread the word that *Ken* was to represent the liberal-labor movement, gloom was the predominant mood in *Ken*'s advertising offices. "No advertising agency, no big business house appeared willing to be on either friendly or commercial terms with a publication that admitted it favored the liberal and labor movement in America. All that the agencies are asking, one of the [advertising] solicitors told me, is that the policy be changed to anti-labor and anti-liberal," George Seldes wrote. It was after the magazine's Chicago department heads came to New York for a banquet and conference with advertising leaders that the purpose of *Ken* began to change. After the meeting, Gingrich called Seldes to his hotel and told him, "They [the advertising men] not only backed me up against the wall, they backed me through the wall."[44] Meyer Levin remembers Smart's attitude after meeting with advertisers. "The publisher had been informed that he had been running a bunch of red magazines featuring a lot of 'Jewish communist' writers. And he had discovered the power of the people who objected to such writings. He had discovered it amongst advertising agency executives."[45]

A day or so later, Smart came to see Seldes, who, at Smart's request, was working on a series about the financial backing for the American Legion.

"Who told you to write those Legion articles?" he shouted. "You did," I [Seldes] replied. "Well, damn it, I've been trying to sign up the Prudential Life for three years; they keep saying *Esquire* isn't their type. So I'm about to land them for *Ken* when you write a piece saying a bunch of bankers formed the Legion and control it, and Franklin D'Olier of the Prudential Life is one of this royal family. We haven't got a chance to get this ad if we run your Legion series." The series is now in the wastebasket.[46]

After that meeting with Smart, Seldes says, the magazine began telling advertisers that *Ken* would be anticommunist as well as antifascist, and circulars and letters containing red-baiting phrases were sent out. Then Gingrich informed Seldes, "The financial winds seem to be blowing the daylights out of that apparently fair-weather form of liberalism that was one of the major tenets of *Ken* as you and I first planned it."[47] So, for the first issue, Seldes was not writing about the press. Nor was he investigating the American Legion. He was preparing a series on the love life of foreign dictators. The pressure from advertisers mounted and advertising dropped, forcing Gingrich to write a convoluted editorial for August 25, 1938, saying that *Ken* was not on the side of labor but saw labor and business working together in a partnership. "Ours is a business civilization. Our empire has been won by enterprise, our ascendancy among nations accomplished to the juggling of dollars rather than the jangling of swords," he wrote, adding at the end that *Ken* was a business enterprise, not a political organ.[48]

Hemingway, Paul de Kruif, George Grosz, Raymond Gram Swing, John L. Spivak, and Seldes were to be listed as "working editors" in *Ken*'s first issue. But, because of red-baiting cartoons, de Kruif resigned on April 18. Spivak told the New York staff of *Ken* as he left for Czechoslovakia that he would resign if red-baiting continued. DeKruif and others cabled Hemingway suggesting he discontinue writing for *Ken*.[49] He didn't. Instead, Hemingway sent Gingrich a letter to be printed in the first issue. It read, "Ernest Hemingway has been in Spain since *Ken* was first projected. Although announced as an editor, he has taken no part in the editing of the magazine or

in the formation of its policies. If he sees eye to eye with us on *Ken*
we would like to have him as an editor. If not he will remain as a
contributor until he is fired or quits."[50] Hemingway probably stayed
with *Ken* because of the amicable relationship he had with Gingrich
and *Esquire*. He continued to contribute to *Ken* through 1938, but
what he wrote was advocacy journalism that served his campaign
for a united front against fascism as well as *Ken*'s need for prominent bylines. By the fourth issue all the "working editors" had been
dropped from the masthead, although some remained as contributors.

Although Gingrich says the antifascist, anticommunist stance had
been the magazine's position from the beginning, it was not listed
as part of any public editorial policy until September 8, 1938, six
months after the magazine began publishing, when a one-paragraph
statement on the table of contents page was printed. The statement
read: "*Ken* . . . A magazine of unfamiliar fact and informed opinion,
filling in the shadows cast by coming events all over the world; equally
opposed to the development of dictatorship from either Left or Right,
whose one fixed editorial aim is to give unhampered and unbiased
demonstration of whatever dangers threaten this democracy from
without and within, in accord with the Lincolnian dictum of, 'Let
the people know the truth and the country is safe.'—Arnold
Gingrich, Editor."[51]

After Seldes was dismissed, Gingrich closeted himself and edited
the magazine alone. At the end of a month he had completed the
first four issues and had two more almost finished. *Ken*'s first issue
had fifty pages of advertising and, for a while, sold an average of
250,000 copies per issue.[52]

Physically, *Ken* was the size of larger magazines like *Esquire*, as
opposed to the smaller standard size of *Time* or the pocketsize *Coronet*. Covers were in full color, most of them painted with an airbrush
by Wesley Neff, an artist who, apparently, is otherwise unknown. The
magazine's nameplate was in a modified script in the upper lefthand
corner. *Ken* was printed on coated, slick paper, and all issues, even
when the advertising dropped to almost nothing, have full-color illustrations inside. Contrast this with issues of *The Nation* and *The
New Republic* for 1938, which are printed on inexpensive newsprint
and have no color illustrations.

There is also a contrast between *Ken*'s advertising content and that of left magazines. On May 19, 1938, *Ken*, with a total of 106 pages, carried 21.3 pages of advertising. *The Nation* and *The New Republic*, which each had a total of 24 pages, had less than 3 pages of advertising, all gathered at the back of the book. It appears that much of *Ken*'s advertising was from *Esquire* clients. There were, for example, full-page, full-color ads for Old Angus Scotch whiskey, Four Roses blended whiskey, Arrow cravats, and Grace Lines. Other advertisers, in black and white, included Eversharp pens, Jameson Irish-American whiskey, *Look* magazine, Talon trouser fasteners, Martell cognac, B and B liquor, Harvey's sherry, and Booth's gin. Although most of these are from the two fields Smart felt wouldn't balk at a political publication, whiskey and men's clothes, there were other ads as well—Phillips milk of magnesia, Lasalle automobiles, Addressograph-Multigraph, Beech Nut gum, and Raymond Whitcomb travel agency—that were independent of the parent magazine. By June 2, advertising dropped to 14 pages and by August 11 to 4.6 pages. The end was near. When, in December, it became apparent that no advertisers would buy the inside back cover of the magazine, *Ken* printed a box score there to show how many predictions made by the magazine had come true.

The magazine, as it finally appeared, did not really seem that leftist. Editorially, *Ken* advocated the use of automobile seat belts, installing parachutes on passenger airlines, and controlling venereal disease by educating women. The magazine exposed the existence of Japanese spies in the Canal Zone, a potential coup in Mexico, and the work of Gestapo agents in Prague.[53] The magazine's writing made few innovations. It was either filled with bombast and outrage, or anonymous "as-told-to" stories from disgruntled bureaucrats or underlings with foreign dictatorships. Much of the writing was breathless, whispered prose, sounding as if the writer either had only a short time to reveal a dark secret or had learned verbal communication from an announcer at a golf tournament. But there was some good writing—including the British correspondence of Claude Cockburn, and, from the May 19, 1938, issue, "The Case of Any Man," by Thompson Young; "Doctors vs. Health," by Lawrence and Sylvia Martin; and "A Measure of Recovery," by John L. Spivak. Still, much of the content of the magazine was scoop-oriented journalism, and time washes away most of its impact. Thirty pages in the center of each issue were devoted to news pictures bought from commercial services like Wide World, International, Globe, Acme, Pix, and International. The illustrations were often insulting—Miriam Hopkins was shown in a picture that made her face look puffy, Katharine Hepburn's picture emphasized her freckles, Claudette Colbert looked chipmunk-faced. As the issues progressed and circulation dropped, the picture pages carried more cheesecake. Articles were illustrated with pictures of scantily clad movie actresses and sultry photos of radio stars that had little to do with the story that accompanied them.

Advertising problems were compounded when, in the third issue, Gingrich ran "Los Angeles Sporting Girl," an article on the life of a prostitute. That, along with a column by Hemingway damning the Catholic Church for its failure to support the Loyalist cause in Spain (the last thing Hemingway would write for an *Esquire*-owned publication), caused the magazine to be denounced in Catholic pulpits across the United States. Priests urged their parishioners to boycott stores that sold any of the three *Esquire*-owned magazines. By midsummer 1939 the boycott had halted *Esquire, Coronet*, and *Ken* sales in fifteen hundred cities or towns. As Meyer Levin remembers it,

> The hallways were hot as the circulation boys ran back and forth with the latest reports from the test town. These figures were terrifying. . . . There was of course an immediate staff order to tone down the contents of the publications, in the hopeful illusion that the sex material was really the source of offense. . . . But the second phase of the campaign now began. Important agencies cancelled advertising. . . . [Smart] made a quick trip to New York. . . . Everything could be straightened out if the policies of the three magazines were rectified. . . . Spain, for instance. There was going to be no more about Spain. That was on the negative side. On the positive side we were going to get some first-class articles on religion, on the Vatican library, things of that kind.[54]

In its struggle for survival, Smart lowered *Ken*'s cover price from a quarter to a dime and started publishing weekly in the spring of

1939. *Ken* limped along until August 1939, when the war in Europe began. In a brief statement to the press after the August 3, 1939, issue, Gingrich said the publishers "were ready to admit they had backed the wrong horse."[55] The eighteen months of *Ken* had cost Smart $404,000. After the death of Smart's political magazine, when it was apparent that *Coronet*'s circulation was slipping and *Verve* was fading into nothing, Gingrich and Albert Smart asked the publisher to promise to live up to a three-year moratorium on new projects. Despite his restless nature and his never-ending schemes for making more money, David Smart agreed.[56] It was time to concentrate on *Esquire* again.

1. *Arnold Gingrich, self-portrait, 1938. Bentley Historical Library, Ann Arbor, Michigan.*

2. *Gaby Smart, unidentified man, David Smart, 1940. Bentley Historical Library, Ann Arbor, Michigan.*

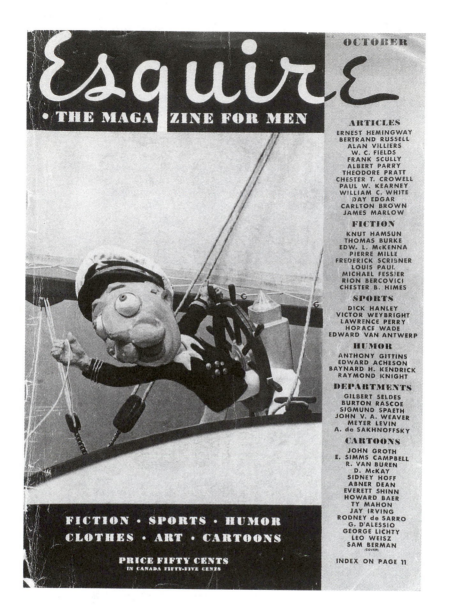

Esquire
• THE MAGAZINE FOR MEN

FICTION • SPORTS • HUMOR
CLOTHES • ART • CARTOONS

PRICE FIFTY CENTS
IN CANADA FIFTY-FIVE CENTS

3. *Esky's smooth sailing.* Esquire *cover, October 1934. The Hearst Corporation.*

4. *Advertisement for Finchley Tuxedos. Note the copy that promises* "absolute correctness." Esquire, *October 1934.*

5. *Advertisement for Manhattan Shirts offering separate collars.* Esquire, *October 1934.*

6. *Cartoon by E. Simms Campbell.* Esquire, *October 1934. The Hearst Corporation.*

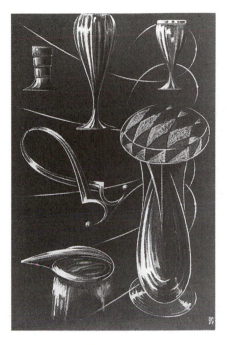

7. *The popularity of streamlined design, which inspired the shape of the Petty Girl and Varga Girl can be seen in this feature in the October, 1934* Esquire. *The Hearst Corporation.*

8. *Fashion illustration from October 1934* Esquire. *The Hearst Corporation.*

BEHOLD THE B.M.O.C. IN A BRAND NEW HAT

9. *Esky Joins the Army. Cover from October 1944* Esquire. *The Hearst Corporation.*

10. Gilbey's Gin advertisement from October 1944 Esquire.

11. Shermund cartoon from October 1944 Esquire. *The Hearst Corporation.*

12. Wartime cartoon by Howard Baer from October 1944 Esquire. *The Hearst Corporation.*

13. Advertisement for Nettleton Shoes promoting the war effort as well as footwear. October 1944 Esquire.

14. *Postwar Esky. Cover from June 1946* Esquire. *The Hearst Corporation.*

*15. Advertisement for Jantzen
bathing suits incorporating the
idea of the Varga Girl pinup.*
Esquire, *June 1946.*

*16. Advertisement for Three
Feathers Whiskey. Postwar product
"at its pre-war best."*

17. *Howard Baer cartoon from June 1946* Esquire. *The Hearst Corporation.*

18. *The postwar look as seen on* Esquire's *fashion pages. From June 1946* Esquire. *The Hearst Corporation.*

19. *Hart Schaffner and Marx advertisement promoting the change from military to civilian fashion.* Esquire, *June 1946.*

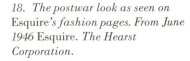

20. *The first Varga Girl, October 1940. The Hearst Corporation.*

21. *The Varga Girl for June 1942. Jeanne Dean, the model for most of the Varga Girl drawings, said this illustration most closely resembled her. The Hearst Corporation.*

PEACE, IT'S WONDERFUL!

When this Military Broad
Blows a toot-a-toota-toot
Is a signal that the Victory is won . . .
And her Soldier Boy returns
After slapping down the Axis
And then leads her to the altar on the run . . .
She will let him slumber homely
When once he wakes to reveille
And sweet-hand him not about his lejune,
But, unless my eyes deceive me,
He won't be so lax, believe me,
When the clock upon their mantel points to "toju!"

PAINTING BY VARGA
VERSE BY PHIL STACK

22. *The Varga Girl at War. April 1943. The Hearst Corporation.*

23. Ken *magazine cover, June 1939.*

6

Vargas, World War II, and All That Jazz

n its sixth anniversary of publication, in December 1939, it looked as if *Esquire* magazine might not last much longer. A year earlier, the magazine had had a circulation of 728,000, but by June 1938 circulation was down almost 40 percent to 453,000. David Smart tried to boost the sagging circulation by doubling the size of the racy Petty Girl drawing to a two-page foldout in December 1939. He added another foldout of a painting by Jean-Gabriel Domergue showing French showgirls at Paris cabarets (several of Domergue's painting were part of a feature called "The World of Pleasure—Le Monde ou L'on S'amuse"), and even included pictures of prize-winning hunting dogs for sportsmen. In all, there were four foldouts in that last issue of the 1930s.

Nothing seemed to work. *Esquire* was not the publishing phenomenon it had once been. Henry Luce and Time, Inc., had started *Life* magazine in 1936, and it, not *Esquire*, became the hot new item on newsstands. *Esquire*'s literary reputation was fading as well. Ernest Hemingway no longer contributed to the magazine, F. Scott Fitzgerald was dead, and Arnold Gingrich's new literary discoveries (Stuart Cloete, Richard Sale, Wolfe Kaufman, Joseph Yablonski, Fritz Leiber, Jr., James Kieran, and Harold Lamb) did not have the luster of the big names he had recruited in the early 1930s. After years of squabbling and being undercut by Smart, William Weintraub left *Esquire* in 1940 and started a public relations agency in New York.

By the April 1940 issue, Smart had changed the magazine's direction. Literature, and everything else, for that matter, took a back seat to sex. The April cover announced, "This issue contains double-sized gatefolds in full color and a cartoon portfolio of 27 extra cartoons." It didn't say much about short stories or articles. By October 1943, there were 63 cartoons in an issue of *Esquire*. Ten years before there had been only 32. And in that same issue there were six pin-ups, five in addition to the gatefold, mostly of Hollywood starlets and chorus girls. The ads that had once announced *Esquire* as a maga-zine of urban self-help now carried the headline, "And this, gentle-men, is what is technically termed a pinup."

Gingrich's dream of a naughty magazine that would tell America's newly urban men how to live was as much a relic of the past as was his editorial control of *Esquire*. In 1937, Smart took the job of se-lecting cartoons away from Gingrich; over the next three years it was the publisher, not the editor, who made all decisions about the magazine's graphic elements.[1] The most popular feature in *Esquire* as the decade changed was the Petty Girl, and Smart meant to capi-talize on it. There was a problem, however. As the offset presses rolled on those three gatefolds for the April issue, George Petty went on strike. When Petty had begun drawing his girls in 1933, he had made one hundred dollars per picture. By the end of the decade his fee had risen to one thousand dollars for each published drawing. He also had the two previously mentioned lucrative advertising ac-counts—Old Gold Cigarettes and Jantzen Swimwear—but he had no contract with *Esquire*. He was holding out for fifteen hundred dol-lars for each Petty Girl painting and the reprint rights to all his work. The Petty Girl did not appear from the April 1940 issue until the beginning of 1941 as Gingrich continued to negotiate with the artist he had discovered in 1932. While negotiations continued, David Smart began searching for a replacement, an artist who could use an airbrush and watercolor technique and was as good as Petty. The search seemed hopeless. Then, in May 1940, a five-foot-two-inch Pe-ruvian artist named Joaquin Alberto Vargas y Chavez showed up un-announced at the magazine's branch office in New York. His paintings were to become the most famous feature ever to run in the pages of *Esquire*.

Alberto Vargas (1896–1982) was born in Arequipa, Peru, five hun-dred miles south of Lima. He was the oldest of the six children of Max and Margarita Vargas. Max Vargas, a photographer best known for his portraits and landscape pictures, had a studio in the Bolivian capital, La Paz, as well as in Arequipa, and Alberto was expected to follow in his father's footsteps. As a child, Alberto learned about cam-eras and lights, negatives and darkroom techniques, and he showed

some skill as an artist—he had been drawing accomplished carica-
tures since he was seven. His father made use of his son's artistic
talent by assigning Alberto the task of retouching negatives with an
airbrush.[2]

In 1911 Max Vargas won a gold medal in Paris for his photographs
of the Inca ruins in the small town of Cuzco. Max Vargas took fourteen-year-old Alberto and his younger brother, Max, Jr., who was
eight, to Paris with him to accept the award. The boys later received
a European education—Alberto in photography and Max in banking. In Paris, the fourteen-year-old Alberto was mesmerized by the
paintings in the museums and galleries, particularly those by Ingres.
But he was also attracted to the sexy drawings of Parisian women by
Raphael Kirchner in the French magazine of Parisian nightlife, *La
Vie Parisienne*. From Paris, his father took him to Zurich, Switzerland, where he studied high school subjects in the suburb of
Rappersville. He read widely and developed an interest in radical labor politics that surfaced from time to time during his career.
Vargas's father returned to Peru, leaving Alberto on his own in Switzerland. In 1915 Alberto moved to Geneva to begin an apprentice-
ship in photography with Julien Studios. A year later, as war engulfed
Europe, his father telegraphed him and told him to relocate in London as the apprentice of Sarony Court Photographers. World War I
conspired against him. He traveled from Geneva to Paris and was
planning to go on to London, but wartime restrictions wouldn't allow him passage. Instead, he bought a ticket to New York, with a
plan to go on to Peru from there. In October 1916, twenty-year-old
Albert Vargas landed for the first time in the United States.[3]

It was not the tall buildings that impressed Vargas that first day
in New York, nor was it the hustle and bustle of commerce. It was
the New York women, emerging from office buildings on their lunch
hour. "From every building came torrents of girls. . . . I had never
seen anything like it," Vargas wrote. "Hundreds of girls with an air
of self-assuredness and determination that said, 'Here I am, how do
you like me?' This certainly was not the Spanish, Swiss, or French
girl!"[4] He decided not to return to Peru, even though his father would
stop all financial support if he stayed in the United States. Vargas's
first New York job was retouching negatives for a commercial photographer. After seven months, he quit and started work for Butterick

Patterns in something of an artistic assembly line: Vargas drew hats and heads and other artists drew legs and shoes for advertisements. In 1917 Vargas sold his first freelance work; later that year he quit his job when he got enough work from magazines and theater and movie advertising to support himself. That same year Vargas met Anna Mae Clift from Soddy (now Soddy-Daisy), Tennessee. She had red hair and blue eyes and was working as a showgirl in *The Green-wich Village Follies* at night and as a fashion model during the day. After a while, Miss Clift, as Vargas called her for years, agreed to pose for him.

By 1919, working with watercolors and airbrush, Vargas was limiting his painting to pretty women, often copying the *art nouveau* style of Kirchner, the magazine illustrator he had discovered eight years before in Paris. In late May Vargas took a job painting a picture of a woman in a Spanish shawl as part of a window display in the Corona Typewriter Building. A group of his paintings was in the background, and people crowded around the window to see the artist, dressed in a smock and beret, and his model at work. On the fifth day of this hot, exhibitionist grind, Sam Kingston, general manager for the *Ziegfeld Follies*, left his card and asked that Vargas bring his samples to Ziegfeld's office the next day. It was Vargas's big break and the start of a twelve-year relationship with the *Follies*. The Broadway producer agreed to pay Vargas two hundred dollars per painting and arranged for stars and showgirls to pose in the artist's fifth-floor walk-up studio. The paintings were used in theater lobbies for publicity.

With the Ziegfeld work came other contracts—a commission from the *New York Tribune* and covers for *Shadowland* (an art magazine), *Motion Picture Weekly,* and Hearst's *American Weekly.* In 1929 he married Anna Mae Clift, who had continued to pose for him during the Ziegfeld years. Although his painting paid well, Vargas spent most of his earnings on books and clothes, and he had to borrow the money for his marriage license. After the *Ziegfeld Follies* closed in 1931, he began painting sexually oriented pictures for Paramount Pictures newspaper advertisements, and in 1934 he landed a contract to paint full-length portraits of movie stars for Hellman's mayonnaise ads. Later that year, Vargas and Anna Mae moved to Hollywood, where he painted a series of portraits of Twentieth Century–Fox stars. Once the portraits were finished, Vargas took a job in the Fox art department but was fired a few months later when Daryl Zanuck took over the studio and installed his own handpicked employees.

Vargas was not out of work for long. During her days as a showgirl, Anna Mae had known the choreographer Busby Berkeley, who was now directing musicals, and she persuaded him to help Vargas get a job in the Warner Brothers art department. He worked as a set designer until 1939. In September of that year Vargas joined a union walkout at Warner Brothers and was subsequently fired and blacklisted as a communist. No other studio would hire him. "We are idealists and that doesn't work in a streamlined age," Anna Mae wrote him in a letter a year later, when he had returned to Manhattan to find work.[5]

At first, New York was no luckier for him than Hollywood had been. Word of a blacklist spreads fast. Anna Mae was near a nervous breakdown from the weight of unemployment, bills, and mortgage payments when Vargas first approached *Esquire*. A week after Vargas showed his samples to the head of the magazine's New York office, David Smart came to town to meet him. It looked as if the publisher had finally found a way to out-Petty the Petty Girl. Vargas went to Chicago with Smart and on June 20, 1940, with Arnold Gingrich as a witness, signed a three-year contract to work for *Esquire*. He was to be paid seventy-five dollars a week, and *Esquire* would own all his artwork. There was one other thing. Smart told Vargas he wanted to call Vargas's paintings "The Varga Girl." Without the final *s* the name sounded so much more "euphonious," Smart said.[6]

Vargas became *Varga*, but this was different from an ordinary name change: *Esquire*, not Alberto Vargas, owned and copyrighted the name Varga. For seventy-five dollars a week, he sold not only his artwork. He sold his name as well. Only 14 out of a total of 180 paintings done for *Esquire* carry Vargas's signature. The rest are stamped with a type logo developed by Smart. At about the same time, Gingrich, who felt Vargas's paintings were "meretricious," reached an agreement for a one-year contract with George Petty.[7] He was to deliver twelve paintings to Esquire to be used during 1941. He would be paid fifteen hundred dollars each. And Petty got to keep his name.

Although some people see little difference between the work of Petty and Vargas, it is only the subject matter that is similar. Petty's

Girls were streamlined, with long legs and frozen smiles. What clothes they wore were often only sketched, giving a feeling of a blueprint—a suggestion of a new model. Although Vargas used some of the same exaggerated anatomical dimensions, he created the appearance of a real woman. In the 1920s and 1930s, Vargas's women were slimmer and more languid than those drawn by Petty. They reflected the influence of the *art nouveau* commercial artists he had seen in Paris—Ralph Kirchner and Maurice Milliere. But by the time he went to work for *Esquire*, the Varga Girls had evolved into full-bodied American beauties who were more Hollywood than Paris, with wholesome, rounded faces, not the high cheekbones of showgirls. As Reid Austin wrote,

> Qualities unique to the Petty Girl . . . were big legs, smiling redundant faces, and action. The artist's particular stylization gave even reflective, quiet poses a taut aura of frozen tension. Tangents abounded. She was designed as a Maserati is designed. Anomalous anatomical aberrations produced a streamlined, enameled equivocation of life. Alberto [Vargas's] creation was, by comparison, trompe l'oeil. One foolishly believed she could exist. Even in action she and her linear composition remained relaxed and utterly feminine.[8]

Artistic styles aside, there was one great similarity between the women drawn by Petty and Vargas. They were consumer items, new products. In an introduction to *Varga: The Esquire Years*, Kurt Vonnegut writes,

> The pinups of World War Two had the generalized appeal of *merchandise*, implied fixed prices and order forms. The fantasy: You really could buy one if you had the bucks, and you just might *have* the bucks someday. . . . About three-quarters of these invented women are blondes or redheads, have no underarm hair or even minor skin blemishes, have legs a third again as long as any woman save for Africa's Watusis. . . . Could I [argue] . . . that the Varga girls were inspired by pornography—or for that

matter, by the varnished nudes in our museums of fine art? I don't think so. Very few women in the pornography or the museums back then seemed to say to their beholders, as do the Varga girls, "I am posing just for *you* at this very moment." A more important consideration: the porn women and the fine arts women were obviously *used* merchandise. The Varga girls, even today and if nothing else, are *new, new, new.* . . . At the same time as I celebrate their imperishable newness, though, I find myself thinking, too, of automobiles fresh off a Michigan assembly line, cars, moreover, which have just been given a coat of the ultimate wax finish. . . . And this wholly inappropriate, often destructive association in the minds of so many of us was conditioned not only by car ads which featured young women, but by the two unrelated things so many of us paired in our thoughts as what we wanted when the war was over: a woman and a motor car. . . . Indeed, as history shows, we often treated our women, when we finally got them and they turned out to be as frailly human as we were, as though they were defective motor cars. A lemon was a lemon, whether a woman or a motor car.[9]

The first Varga Girl appeared in the October 1940 issue of *Esquire.* She was an immediate hit. The magazine's new feature was promoted with direct mail advertising, house ads in *Esquire,* and window cards at newsstands. Then Smart decided on a Varga Girl calendar similar to the one featuring the Petty Girl that Old Gold cigarettes had offered as a premium the year before. Vargas rushed out twelve additional paintings, and they were printed in the December 1940 issue. *Esquire* also offered the calendar for sale through mail order. It sold 325,000 copies at a quarter each. The Varga Girl was on the way to becoming an industry, not just a magazine feature. The sale of the first Varga calendar prompted *Esquire* to open a separate division— Esquire Buy-Products—which merchandised, in addition to the calendars, Varga playing cards, Varga datebooks, and Varga yearbooks. Vargas got only his salary. The profits from the buy-items went to *Esquire.*

Initially, Vargas repainted some of his old work for *Esquire* because of deadline pressure and because David Smart wanted it revised to be as much like the Petty Girl as possible. Although Vargas's publicity said he worked only from memory, he usually had his wife as a model. Smart killed those early paintings because he felt Anna Mae's body was too athletic. Vargas's search for another model lead him to a fifteen-year-old red-haired girl named Jeanne Dean, an usherette at the Studio Theater in downtown Chicago, where she wore a smock and beret to escort patrons to their seats. She lied about her age to get the job, which called for blondes or redheads between five foot two and five five and eighteen years old or older. On a bus ride between high school and the theater, Jeanne Dean met a Chicago artist, Shirley Friend, who tried to hire her as a model for a painting of the American melting pot that included a typical American girl. Dean's mother was dating an FBI agent, and she talked him into running a background check on Friend. When the artist proved to be legitimate, Dean posed for her wearing a sweater and skirt.

Friend knew Vargas, who, at that time, before his *Esquire* paintings had been published, was an unknown artist, and suggested Dean model for him. Dean and her mother traveled to Vargas's apartment where they met Alberto, Anna Mae, and David and Alfred Smart. Dean was terrified of the Smarts, who told her she could have no publicity for her work because *Esquire* didn't want the public to know Vargas used models. So from 1940 to 1943 Jeanne Dean, wearing leotards, bathing suits, shorts, flimsy negligees, and folded drapes, modeled for Vargas at his apartment. She never posed nude during those years. Each session lasted two or three hours, and she earned fifty cents an hour. It would take three or four sessions for Vargas to complete a painting. During the years she was the Vargas model, Dean would meet people who would say, "You look so familiar to me." But she never told them why. Anna Mae Vargas, who was at all the sessions, apologized to Dean for the low pay and said they'd try to make it up to her some day. It seemed to Dean that the Vargases were so close they were actually one person, with Alberto doing the painting and Anna Mae handling everything else. She remembers Alberto as being, "a naive, humble little guy."[10]

Smart called Vargas "young man" and treated Alberto and Anna Mae like children, instructing them to call him "Uncle David," although the publisher was only four years older than the artist. He helped the artist and his wife pick out an apartment on Lake Shore Drive near the *Esquire* offices and instructed them on the proper furnishings. Smart also told the Vargases that if they needed any extra money, all they had to do was ask, and he'd have the *Esquire* accounting department issue a check. What he didn't say was that the extra money was an advance against earnings. Smart was, in effect, running a company store. Vargas never got a statement from *Esquire*, and by December 1944 he owed the magazine $5,395.[11]

Both the Petty Girl and the Varga Girl appeared in *Esquire* during the twelve months of 1941, but Smart devoted all his attention to promoting the Varga product. He got advertising contracts for Vargas as well. Varga Girls began appearing in ads for MGM, Twentieth Century–Fox, Jantzen swimsuits, Acme beer, the Sealy Mattress Company, Raymond Laboratories, Jergen's face powder, and Cool Ray Permanent Wave hair products. Initially, the Varga Girl was listed in the *Esquire* table of contents as "poetry," because the painting accompanied verse by Phil Stack, an *Esquire* staff writer. The first Varga Girl, wearing a skintight one-piece bathing suit so sheer her nipples could be seen through it, was shown talking on the phone while lying back on the bed. The poem accompanying it reads

Irene, I just called up
to let you know
That I am signing off that guy from Butte,
Though his intentions may be pure as snow
The way that cowboy rhumbas isn't cute!
He says it's pretty lonely in New York
And here is one for Ripley to endorse—
The other night when we were at the Stork
He called up home and asked about his
    HORSE!

What's that you say . . . for me to hold on tight?
Speak louder! This connection isn't clear. . . .
Oh, Boy! You're sure that Winchell has it right?
SIX SILVER MINES! How interesting, my Dear!
As RICH as THAT? He surely doesn't show it. . . .
MY GOD! I've been in love and didn't know it.

It was a variation on the old chorus-girl-as-gold digger theme that had been so popular when *Esquire* was first published. But, as Smart would find out, the nation's idea of glamour had moved from New York to Hollywood, even though Stack's poem hadn't, and it was the time Vargas spent working on advertisements for motion pictures and designing sets for the studios that gave him the understanding of what American men saw as sex appeal. And American women too, for that matter. One-fourth of Vargas's fan mail was from women who wanted to know how they could look more like the Varga Girl.[12] Vargas may have started out as an illustrator for the *Ziegfeld Follies*, but he knew it was images from the movies, not the showgirl in Phil Stack's verse, that gave America its ideal of feminine charm in 1940.

In *American Beauty*, Lois Banner's book on the perception of feminine beauty in America, the author says independent, square-shouldered women were the ideal in the 1940s, and she cites Rosalind Russell and Joan Crawford as examples. She overlooks Rita Hayworth and Betty Grable, the two most glamorous Hollywood pinups of the decade. And she never mentions the Varga Girl. Later, Banner writes, "Where the sensual woman of the 1930s had been moderately curved and often upper class in style, the voluptuous woman of the 1950s was huge-bosomed and, as portrayed by Ava Gardner or Jane Russell, of indeterminate, lower-class origin. 'Mammary goddesses' one scholar has called them."[13]

The new cinematic standard of beauty in the 1950s did not come from nowhere. It was a real-life extension of the imaginary women in the Vargas paintings of the 1940s, who were first portrayed on the screen by a dozen models in a special Varga Girl sequence in the 1942 MGM film *DuBarry Was a Lady*. Hollywood actresses who were an extension of the Varga Girl include, in addition to Gardner and Russell, Rhonda Flemming, Maureen O'Hara, Marilyn Monroe, Diana Dors, Debra Paget, Janet Leigh, Lizabeth Scott, Virginia Mayo, Terry Moore, and Lana Turner. Even Jeanne Dean, the prototype for the Varga Girl, appeared for a while in Hollywood movies. Vargas may have begun his career copying the image of Ziegfeld girls, but by the mid-1940s he had created a look of his own—busty, usually blonde or red-haired, long-legged, superficially wholesome, and sultry—that Hollywood patterned its stars after. He became the creator, and the real girls from the glamorous studios were his copies. The Varga Girl's appeal was not limited to Hollywood. In the mid-1940s, the girlie shows on American midways used the Varga Girl as a sure ticket seller. A burlesque impresario named Joe Kara presented a show under canvas across the nation called "*Esquire* Girls" that used paintings of Varga-like women on banners that promised "Burlesque Beauties," "Du Barrys On Parade," "Can Can Cuties," "French Follies," "Seductive Charmers," and "Paris After Midnight." The banner carried the *Esquire* script logo, probably without permission.[14]

One of the first signs that the Varga Girl was becoming an American phenomena was in *The New Yorker* "Talk of the Town" feature for January 11, 1941:

> Uncertain of the future, but fearing the worst, we read a prospectus about the 1941 calendar that *Esquire* is urging on its readers—a dozen pages of nepenthe, each illustrated by Varga, an artist who could make a girl look nude if she were rolled up in a rug. "Order it, look at it, feel it quiver; set it to the music of a slow drum roll," said the announcement. "The Varga Calendar, festooned with girls faultless in limb and shaping, girls curved with strange magics, girls of eggshell smoothness and the warmth of monsoons, has been printed in the full, lush colors of life—to bring you pulsing dreams throughout each siesta and vigil of the passing year . . . its heartening message, spelled with the turn of a thigh or the lift of a hip." This may be just the thing we need right now. A little concentration and perhaps we can visualize each month as a separate and lovely encounter with a beautiful stranger, the whole year as a harmless and joyous trip through the old seraglio. It is nice to think of *Esquire* readers joyfully awaiting the turning of each page, identifying each four weeks with a new delight. Skipping ahead, we are now in a position to tell you what is in store for you. August, the invasion month, is a cutie lying prone on a beach, covered slightly by a transparent hat. October, when the sky may be full of bombers, is a slip of a girl bared from toe to hip, shooting an arrow. November, when the mists may be

rolling over the Channel, perhaps as a shroud, will be a blonde in a dress as tight and as white as the skin over the knuckles of our fist. What may be the end of the world will be marked by a nice thigh, the beginning of chaos by the lift of a pretty hip. That's the year ahead of you, gentlemen. Feel it quiver. Set it to the music of a slow drum.[15]

The imaginary Varga Girl was poised against the grim reality of the approaching horror of World War II. But that war would make her more popular than ever.

In December 1941, just as the last Petty Girl and the second Varga Girl calendar were being readied for the newsstand, the Japanese bombed Pearl Harbor. Within a week, America was at war. For some American entrepreneurs, including David Smart, World War II was a gold mine. Robert Woodruff, the president of Coca-Cola, had his product declared a morale booster. He persuaded the army and navy that his five-cent beverage was an essential product and should not be subject to the rationing quotas that would have prevented Coca-Cola from obtaining the sugar it needed. He also persuaded the military that a Coca-Cola bottling plant should follow the soldiers into combat. So, as the war progressed, factories for America's best-known product were carried throughout Europe as the skeleton for what would become a worldwide bottling network. Just as shrewd was Phillip K. Wrigley, the chewing gum magnate, who had his product listed as an essential wartime commodity. Like Woodruff, Wrigley needed sugar for his product to survive. And like the Coca-Cola executive, he knew that if it were declared an essential commodity, he would not be subject to sugar rationing. Wrigley supplied a stick of his chewing gum in each package of combat rations the military produced after he had persuaded the Subsistence Research Laboratory of Chicago that his product would relieve thirst, keep a soldier's mouth moist, act as a tobacco substitute, and clean teeth. Neither Woodruff nor Wrigley made much profit on wartime manufacturing, but both Coca-Cola and Wrigley's chewing gum stayed on the market during a period of severe rationing while some similar products vanished.[16]

David Smart didn't need sugar; he was supplying sugar-coating. It was not sugar rationing he had to overcome, but a shortage of paper. Smart convinced the military that a magazine filled with pin-ups, racy cartoons, and camp humor was essential for military mo-rale. Other magazines declared morale boosters were *The Reader's Digest* and *Life*. The War Production Board gave each magazine pub-lishing company a paper allocation based on weight. Most magazines cut back on either page size or number of pages. *Esquire* had another idea. Arnold Gingrich persuaded Smart to buy lighter-weight paper. The company switched from fifty-pound to twenty-pound stock, and by using cheaper paper—the twenty-pound paper was little more than newsprint—*Esquire* was able to keep its prewar size and also have enough paper left over to print *Coronet*, whose circulation was growing beyond its allotment.[17] Gingrich called the newsprint "ABCD paper," for almanacs, bibles, concordances, and dictionaries, and tried to convince advertisers it was not a second-class product.[18]

By 1943, with a circulation of more than 600,000, *Esquire* was sell-ing 69,000 subscriptions to servicemen, and another 30,000 copies were sold to post exchanges to be distributed to military bases in Europe. An additional 100,000 copies of a special military edition of *Esquire*, printed without advertising, were distributed free to troops. *Esquire* was one of the three magazines most requested by servicemen. The other two were *Life*, which carried the original ver-sions of the famous pinup photographs of Rita Hayworth in bed (Au-gust 11, 1941) and the Betty Grable backside (1942), and *The Reader's Digest*. Originally, the advertising-free military edition of *Esquire* was to be printed in a miniature edition, like the ones pub-lished by *Time, Newsweek*, and *The New Yorker*, but the Special Ser-vices Division of the Armed Forces requested the magazine full-size because soldiers didn't want miniature Varga Girls.[19] Paper for the military edition was over and above the allotment from the War Pro-duction Board. Then there were the *Esquire* Buy-Products. In 1941, the Varga Girl calendar sold 325,000 copies; by 1944 sales were up to 2.5 million calendars. Of the 300,000 copies of the 1943 calendar sold by mail, 49 percent were shipped to servicemen. In addition, *Esquire* offered a military reprint package of its pinups and cartoons for five dollars. More than 1,000 of those were sold.[20]

In effect, the United States government was *Esquire*'s biggest cus-tomer, accounting for 200,000 copies of its magazines (including the military edition) and 49 percent of calendar sales. And just as David

Smart was unwilling to upset piano makers and bankers who might advertise, he was certainly not going to violate government standards in *Esquire*. Those standards came from different branches of the bureaucracy. In his efforts to sell war bonds, Henry Morgenthau, Jr., secretary of the treasury, opposed a bond sales booth at Rockefeller Plaza because "that's the place where they sell the most precious jewelry and high-priced furs." He suggested female billboard models who were not "Hollywood actresses swathed in mink," but girls from the International Ladies' Garment Workers' Union "swathed in overalls."[21] The Varga Girl was made to fit the Morgenthau ideal. After the 1940 versions of Vargas's creation, which showed nipples and buttock cleavage, there were only three instances of nudity from 1941 to 1946. The haughty, upper-class faces changed to more wholesome, apple-cheeked American girls who posed in bathing suits, grass skirts, abbreviated WAC uniforms, Navy shirts, a towel, evening gowns, cowgirl suits, maid's uniforms, and, only occasionally, a negligee. The Varga Girl (who was drawn to look twenty-five years old) may not have been swathed in overalls, but she certainly abandoned mink coats, showgirl costumes, and expensive jewelry. It is true, as *The New Yorker* wrote, that Vargas could make a woman look nude if she were rolled in a rug, but the women he drew began to conform to the ideals of Henry Morgenthau.

It may seem odd that *Esquire*, a magazine filled with pinups and cartoons, was considered a morale booster during World War II, but the morale boost it offered to servicemen was not much different from the wartime efforts of Hollywood and the motion picture industry, whose leaders decided that entertainment was among the many things that could build morale. Walt Disney made cartoons of dancing red corpuscles, Myrna Loy began spending the afternoons in her movies at a Red Cross class, not playing bridge, and Bob Hope started telling jokes about the national rubber shortage. The movies were mostly the same as before the war, but with different costumes—military uniforms instead of business suits—and villains became Gestapo members or German or Japanese soldiers rather than American Indians. *Esquire* responded in much the same way. Varga Girls either dressed like George Washington and brandished swords or wore military uniforms and sheer patriotic garments in red, white, and blue; cartoons featured soldiers, not men-about-town, and the girls were often in uniform as well; two full pages of "camp humor," risqué jokes sent in by servicemen, were added to the magazine. It was the same *Esquire* that was revamped in 1939, only now it was camouflaged in olive drab. Maybe the change can best be seen in Phil Stack's poems. In 1940, he wrote about gold diggers. By February 1942, his verse was a call to arms:

> We go to war for many precious things. . . .
> But first of all for freedom that we prize,
> And we will guard with fighting ships and wings
> This girl who lives beneath Hawaiian skies;
> And he who struck behind a peaceful word
> Will find the Eagle swoops to stalk its prey. . . .
> America has wakened and is stirred!
> America is on the march today!

To an American serviceman, America was Coca-Cola, Double Mint, and Varga Girls. Or, as comedian Bob Hope said in a segment of a World War II newsreel, "Our American troops are ready to fight at the drop of an *Esquire*."[22] Kurt Vonnegut saw military advantages in the Varga Girl:

> The American male's capacity to make do with imaginary women gave our military forces a logistical advantage I have never seen acknowledged anywhere. Commanders of other armies and navies had to try to arrange, however cumbersomely and often cruelly, for some sort of female companionship, in a manner of speaking, for their fighters from time to time. But American soldiers and sailors simply brought their own undemanding and nearly weightless paper dolls along.[23]

The Varga Girls were more than paper dolls, however. They were a representation of home. And home was what most soldiers were fighting for—not democracy or liberty. They wanted a chance to go back to their jobs, houses, wives, girlfriends, and automobiles. In *V Was for Victory*, John Morton Blum analyzes the yearnings of the American GI:

The Germans and the Japanese, the targets of heroic striving, were dragons to be slain, after which the hero could return to his fair lady in her fair land. The content of heroic imagery said little about freeing the oppressed, an objective to which some Union soldiers had given high priority eighty years earlier, or about making the world safe for democracy, the stirring purpose of so many doughboys in 1918. The hero of World War II stood for blueberry pie and blond sweethearts, for the family farm and for Main Street, for perseverance and decency—for Americanism as a people's way of being. Brave men, those heroes, and nice guys, too, but it was in the folk culture of the national past, ebullient still in their own day, that they fought for their brave new world.[24]

There was no blueberry pie on the battlefield, but, in the form of the Varga Girl, there were plenty of blonde sweethearts. Like a seminude figurehead from a nineteenth-century sailing ship, the Varga Girl was emblazoned on the noses of aircraft, the sides of tanks, and the bows of ships. She became the symbol of home, a popular-culture keepsake.[25]

Much of the World War II morale boosting originated with the Office of Wartime Information, which was controlled by Madison Avenue advertising men like Bruce Barton, the author of *The Man Nobody Knows* (a biography of Jesus as the first great salesman and the best cocktail party guest in Jerusalem); and Gardner Cowles, Jr., the publisher of *Look* magazine. Both said advertising was a crucial element in winning the war and urged corporations to place institutional advertising in newspapers and magazines in an effort to keep American morale up. The advertising meant that companies with few products to sell because of wartime shortages would continue to buy space and publications would turn a profit. "He's hard on shoes . . . you can't afford to be," says an *Esquire* ad for Florsheim Shoes that shows an American soldier crawling on his belly through the Pacific jungle. In other *Esquire* advertising, a headline screamed, "Fire Power Makes the Kill," to promote the Oldsmobile division of General Motors; "Loose Talk Can Cost Lives," said the copy above a full-color picture of the Sphinx wearing a fashionable men's hat. "Keep It Under Your Stetson." There was also a full-page message from Wilson Sports Equipment, written by L. B. Icely, the president of the company, that urged,

> Let us resolve from this war on, America shall be *a physically fit, ever-ready people*. First—let us see that our returning fighters are *kept* in good condition. . . . Let there be more golf clubs, more tennis and badminton courts, more play fields and gymnasiums. . . . Let us . . . be a *Nation of Athletes*—ever-ready, if need be, to sustain our rights by the might of millions of physically fit sports-trained, freedom-loving Americans.

With advertising men in charge of the Office of War Information, the war itself became a product, not a cause. "Step right up and get your delicious four freedoms," wrote Henry Pringle while he was working for the Office of Wartime Information in a parody of Coca-Cola and Madison Avenue's War efforts. "It's a refreshing war."[26]

The government not only accounted for 200,000 issues of *Esquire* and encouraged much of its advertising, it was also determining men's fashions in a way the magazine itself had done in prewar days. In March 1942, the War Production Board issued an order for bidding men's suits to include an extra pair of pants, fancy backs, pleats, patch pockets, or cuffs. A vest could be offered only with single-breasted suits. The order also called for the manufacture of single-breasted suits with shorter jackets and narrow lapels. Zoot suits were forbidden. This new fashion code, the War Production Board believed, would save 40 to 50 million pounds of wool a year. *Esquire's* fashion editor, O. E. Schoeffler, endorsed the changes. "The required narrower trousers without cuffs conform to a good standard of dress," he wrote. "These have been noted and illustrated in the fashion pages of *Esquire*, particularly in connection with the return of Simple Elegance. . . . All in all, more men will dress in accordance with good fashion standards as a result of these rulings."[27] *Esquire* also indirectly endorsed another fashion change. In 1943, the War Production Board ordered a 10 percent reduction in the amount of cloth in women's bathing suits. The short "bathing skirts" of the 1930s were banished, and there was a concentration on two-piece bathing suits because of the savings in the cloth that would no longer be needed to cover the midriff. The Varga Girl complied with the ruling. After August 1943, when dressed for the beach, she only appeared in two-piece bathing suits.

Although the editorial content of the magazine was addressed to young GIs, the advertising in *Esquire* was targeted at an older market. GIs slogging through Italy or the jungles of the Pacific wore government-issued uniforms. The latest fashion trend meant little to them. So fashion ads appealed to the man left behind. In October 1943, the copy from a Hart Schaffner and Marx advertisement read, "Every month he's on the dot with that 10 per cent for war bonds. Every day he's on the job, tackling the problems of a busy war plant v.p. For the latter role he likes the easy comfort of Pan-American shetlands." The illustration is of a businessman with gray temples. An ad for Alpagora overcoats features a gray-haired professor lecturing a friend of the same age about the value and quality of the product; Nettleton Shoes shows a middle-aged father in fashionable civilian clothes shaking hands with his young son, who wears an army uniform; Portis Hats makes its pitch with gray-haired men dressed in "victory styles." Any advertising featuring younger men is for custom-tailored military uniforms like Mid City Uniform Cap Company, Swank Men's Jewelry, or Paris Garters and Free-Swing Suspenders. Advertising for liquor features older men as well. Lord Calvert shows "the man of decision," in his fifties, drinking a hi-ball and Kinsey Blended Whiskey shows two aging civil defense workers enjoying a cocktail, while Seagram's Seven Crown features a painting of two graying men with developing double chins toasting each other. Most of the liquor ads carried a caveat like this one from Four Roses: "We are trying to apportion our pre-war stocks to assure you a continuing supply until the war is won. Meanwhile, our distilleries are devoted 100% to the production of alcohol for explosives, rubber and other war products." Unlike Wrigley's chewing gum and Coca-Cola, whiskey was not a government-sanctioned morale booster.

Aside from the war, there were changes in popular culture on the home front, particularly in music. And Arnold Gingrich, who was still *Esquire*'s editor although much of his authority had been usurped by Smart, was having bad luck picking authors. Part of the reason was Smart's insistence that *Esquire* fiction act as a morale booster so the magazine could keep its military distribution. Gingrich fared much better by devoting pages of *Esquire* to new trends in jazz. The magazine published its first work on jazz in 1934, when Charles Edward Smith, the author of *Jazzmen*, a book about New Orleans musicians, wrote "Collecting Hot," an article about how to collect jazz records. Gingrich had little interest in jazz at the time, but on one of his trips to New York in the early 1940s, he stopped at a record store near Grand Central Station and overheard an old recording of Louis Armstrong playing "West End Blues." He was hooked and began collecting jazz records. Soon after that, in 1943, jazz began showing up regularly in *Esquire*.[28]

There was some controversy in the early 1940s about just what jazz was. Swing, which to most *Esquire* readers meant all-white big bands like the ones conducted by Glenn Miller, Harry James, Kay Kyser, Tommy and Jimmy Dorsey, and Artie Shaw, was the backbone of the nation's popular music. The Swing Era started in 1934 when Benny Goodman, who hired Fletcher Henderson, a black musician, to write arrangements for his orchestra, played for a year at the Billy Rose Music Hall in New York and had a network radio show. Although Goodman popularized swing for white audiences, the form was actually developed by Henderson, who had one of America's first big bands. He, along with musicians like Fats Waller, originated the style Goodman made famous. In the 1940s, swing was considered a category of its own and jazz was something else. Some listeners thought jazz was any "hot" music played by a small group. The use of the word *hot* came from Paris where, in 1932, Hugues Panassie opened Le Club Hot, or, as it became known, the Hot Club of France. Other fans, later known as Moldy Figs, contended that jazz was only New Orleans music, or Dixieland. Whatever jazz was, any understanding was further complicated by the American Federation of Musician's recording ban, which would not allow union members to play on recordings. The ban was an effort to raise musicians' salaries; James E. Petrillo, the union president, felt recorded music was taking money away from live musicians and believed musicians should be paid more for records that would be played over and over again. The ban lasted from August 1942, until November 1944. During those years, the only new records made were by vocal groups (the Andrews Sisters, the Ink Spots) who sang without instrumental accompaniment. So when *Esquire* ran its first All-American Band issue in February 1943, there was some confusion about what kind of band it would be.

Gingrich's original idea was to name an All-American band the way *Collier's* magazine named an All-American football team each fall. To write the article, he chose Robert Goffin, a Belgian (1898–1984) who immigrated to the United States in 1940. In Belgium, Goffin had been a prominent criminal lawyer, a poet, and the author of books on gastronomy, natural history, and legal finance. In 1927 he became editor of *Music*, the Belgian jazz magazine, and in 1932 wrote *Aux Frontiers du Jazz*, a book that urged readers to go beyond Paul Whiteman and Bing Crosby to understand the American music form. Goffin was a prominent antifascist and escaped to Portugal in 1940 after his country was invaded by Germany. He left behind more than three thousand jazz records, as well as paintings by Renoir, Gauguin, and Modigliani.[29] Once in New York, Goffin, a big man over six feet tall and weighing more than 250 pounds, worked with English jazz critic Leonard Feather, who had come to the United States from London in 1935 after working in a minor job for British Lion film studios and writing for *Melody Maker, Gramophone, Tune Times*, the *Era*, and *Swing Time*. Together, Goffin and Feather planned the first American course on the history of jazz. It was taught, beginning in 1942, at the New School for Social Research in Greenwich Village.

Goffin and Feather met Arnold Gingrich in 1943 at a nightclub called The Hurricane where they listened to a Duke Ellington concert. The three of them began making plans for *Esquire*'s jazz poll, which would be published for the first time in 1944. Both Goffin and Feather suggested that a panel of experts pick the All-American band rather than have the choice made by a readers' poll. A readers' poll, they feared, would result in an all-white band and because of the recording ban would ignore much of the innovative jazz being played in New York (mostly in clubs on West Fifty-second Street, or "Swing Street," as it was called).[30] The first *Esquire* jazz panel included, in addition to Feather and Goffin, E. Simms Campbell, the *Esquire* cartoonist; George Avakian, a jazz record producer; Abel Green, the editor of *Variety*; Elliott Grennard, a writer for *Billboard*; John Hammond, a record producer; Roger Kay, an Egyptian critic writing in the United States for *Orchestra World*; Harry Lim, a Javanese organizer of jam sessions; Paul Eduard Miller, a regular *Esquire* contributor; Bucklin Moore, author of *The Darker Brother*; Timmie Rosenkrantz, editor of a Danish swing magazine; Charles Edward Smith, the author of *Jazzmen*; Frank Stacy, New York editor of *Downbeat*; Bob Thiele, editor of *Jazz* magazine; and Barry Ulanov, editor of *Metronome*.

Winners of the first "Esky" awards (small gold and silver statues of the popeyed *Esquire* corporate symbol) included Louis Armstrong, trumpet; Jack Teagarden, trombone; Benny Goodman, clarinet; Coleman Hawkins, saxophone; Art Tatum, piano; Al Casey, guitar; Oscar Pettiford, bass; Sid Catlett, drums; Red Norvo and Lionel Hampton, tied for miscellaneous instrument; Louis Armstrong, male vocalist; Billie Holliday, female vocalist; and Artie Shaw, best musician in the armed forces. The African American press hailed the poll results with banner headlines: "20 of 26 Winning Musicians in *Esquire* Band Poll Are Negroes," announced the *Amsterdam News*; "'Ace' Negro Musicians Sweep *Esquire* Mag's Jazz Band Poll," read the headline in the Pittsburgh *Courier*. The white jazz press was not so enthusiastic. *Jazz Record*, edited by the pianist Art Hodes, called the results "inverted Jim Crow" and said they were a "foul and dismal smirch" on the reputations of the critics who chose the winners. In *The Record Changer* Ralph J. Gleason, a San Francisco jazz critic, objected to the poll because he felt it ignored the real jazz of New Orleans in favor of swing music, which he said wasn't jazz at all.[31]

Gingrich thought of the poll only as a magazine article; David Smart saw it as a great promotion. The winners were presented in concert at the Metropolitan Opera House in New York, the first jazz concert ever played from that stage. The concert was a benefit for the Navy League, and there was a booth in the lobby selling War Bonds. More than $600,000 were raised. The show was broadcast nationwide and recorded to be broadcast later over the Armed Forces Network. (The recording ban did not include records made for use by the military.) For the next few years, *Esquire* was the only major magazine in the country promoting jazz. In addition to its All-American band and other articles that appeared each February through 1947, *Esquire* published an annual *Jazz Book* including articles, discographies, and biographies about the poll winners. In 1945 a "New

Stars" division was added, and through that category bebop musicians Dizzy Gillespie and Charlie Parker got some of their first national publicity. *Esquire*'s jazz emphasis even inspired Coleman Hawkins to record songs titled "*Esquire* Bounce" and "*Esquire* Blues."

"*Esquire* Blues" was probably an appropriate title for that era. Although the magazine was considered a morale booster by the armed forces, another branch of the government, the U.S. Post Office, was trying to have *Esquire* closed down because it was obscene. To defend itself against those charges, the magazine was to spend four years in court.

7

Esky Goes to Court

n October 1942, as *Esquire* recovered from its prewar slump, David Smart got married. His wife, a tall blonde who towered over him, was a former Ziegfeld Girl. Her name was Edna Richards, and she called herself Gabrielle Dure, but everyone knew her as Gaby. After leaving Ziegfeld, Gaby Dure moved to Chicago and went to work as a fashion model at Stanley Korshak's clothing store, across from the Drake Hotel on North Michigan Avenue. She was introduced to Smart in 1935 by Freeman Gosden, who played Amos on the *Amos 'n' Andy* radio show. For seven years Smart courted Gaby Dure, sending her on trips to Europe with Gingrich and his wife, showering her with gifts. But he was reluctant to marry her because she was not Jewish.[1] On the eve of his fiftieth birthday, he changed his mind and they were married. It was sometimes a stormy relationship, with Smart yelling at Dure in public and making decisions for her about clothes, jewelry, and travel.[2]

Once married, Smart moved from his penthouse apartment to a mansion in suburban Glenview. Designed by Howard Van Doren Shaw, the house overlooked the eleventh hole of the exclusive Glenview Club.[3] Domestic bliss was not Smart's style, and he used the new mansion in two moneymaking schemes. First, he became enamored of roses and put rose-scented ads in *Esquire* to promote plants grown by his gardener, Walter Domke. Smart expanded the business beyond his backyard and bought the Willowbrook Nursery to grow and sell his roses. If *Esquire* readers wanted to say it with roses, they evidently got them from the florist, not from their own bushes; as a horticultural entrepreneur, Smart was a flop.

Then the publisher decided he wanted his own movie studio. On a prewar trip to Germany, Smart was impressed with educational films developed by the German army, particularly one showing how to shoot a rifle. He became convinced that his future was in educational films.[4] He cleared part of the wooded lot behind his mansion, to the dismay of his neighbors, and built a movie studio designed to turn out one educational film a week. His company was called Coronet Instructional Films and, like his rose business, it was a financial failure. The company had to be taken over by *Esquire* to bail Smart out of debt. The navy took over operations of the studio during the war to make training films. After the war, however, under Smart's management Coronet Films became successful in producing classroom documentaries.

Meanwhile, back at the magazine, Arnold Gingrich was becoming involved in six years of harassment from the U.S. Post Office. Beginning with the January 1941 issue, each issue of *Esquire* was submitted to the solicitor of the post office for approval. This was not standard operating procedure for the post office: other magazines didn't have to submit issues for approval. If any feature was deemed objectionable by post office officials, Gingrich would change it. By 1942, the editor was bringing batches of cartoons to Washington for approval.

In his memoirs, Gingrich writes of the beginning of the post office investigation into *Esquire*:

> In the Spring of 1942 we began having trouble with the Post Office Department over the moral tone of *Esquire*. Our first communications with the department were all with its solicitor, Vincent Miles, and before long I was making monthly trips to Washington, taking the dummy of the next issue of *Esquire* to go to press, and going over it page by page, and particularly cartoon by cartoon, to get his clearance prior to publication. I hated doing it . . . but it seemed the only safe way to stay out of trouble. I would make all the required revisions on the spot, and some of the things I had to "tone down" seemed to be a case of bending over backwards to avoid offending even the most sensitive of sensibilities to a degree that was nearly ludicrous.[5]

But even the monthly trips to Washington from *Esquire*'s offices in Chicago and the changes made to satisfy the censors were not enough for the post office. Over Labor Day weekend of 1943, Frank Walker, the postmaster general, cited *Esquire* to show cause why its second-class mailing privileges (cheaper mailing rates granted to magazines) should not be withdrawn. If *Esquire* lost that privilege, the magazine's mailing expenses would go up four hundred thousand dollars a year, a cost that could put the publication out of business.[6]

Frank Walker, a confidant of President Franklin Roosevelt, became postmaster general after James A. Farley, Roosevelt's first campaign manager, resigned from the position to protest the president's decision to run for a third term. Walker and his family moved from Pennsylvania to Montana in 1889, when he was three. He spent his boyhood as a grocery store delivery boy, attended Gonzaga University in Spokane, Washington, from 1903 to 1906, and received an LL.B. from Notre Dame in 1909. He was elected assistant district attorney of Silver Bay County, Montana, the same year he graduated from law school, and he held that job through 1912. In 1913 he was elected to the state legislature and formed, with his brother, the law firm of Walker and Walker. His list of clients soon included John D. Ryan, head of Anaconda Copper Company. Walker soon became Ryan's chief aide. In 1925 Walker moved to New York to be general counsel and manager of Comfort Theaters, Incorporated, a chain of move theaters owned by his uncle. In less than twenty years Walker had moved from his working-class origins to the heady world of corporate leadership. He contributed ten thousand dollars to Roosevelt's New York gubernatorial reelection campaign in 1928, thus beginning his relationship with the future president. Four years later, when Roosevelt first ran for president, Walker became a fundraiser and contributed another ten thousand dollars to the New York governor. The same year, after Roosevelt was nominated, Walker was elected treasurer of the Democratic National Committee.

When Roosevelt took office, Walker was named executive secretary of the Executive Council, a group that acted as contact point between the cabinet and newly created recovery agencies. Six months later, in December 1933, he was made head of the National Emergency Council. Walker was dissatisfied with his work in government, however, and returned to the theater business in 1934. He returned to government one more time with the National Relief Agency, found that unappealing, and by 1936 was back in private business. He was again a fundraiser for the Roosevelt Memorial Library in 1938 and became part of an inner circle that shaped strategy for the 1940 third-term campaign. He became chairman of the Democratic National Committee and then, on August 31, 1940, was appointed postmaster general.

Walker was one of the wealthiest men connected with the New Deal, one of the most conservative of Roosevelt's advisors, and an ardent and influential Roman Catholic who was prominent in Catholic charity work.[7] In November 1941, Walker accompanied Catholic Bishop James E. Welch to a meeting with the Japanese ambassador to the United States; at the meeting he promised that the U.S. would resume oil exports if Japan would withdraw from Indochina.[8]

Walker's high connections with the Catholic Church and his conservatism started him on a censorship binge. In his first two years as postmaster general he cited twenty-three magazines as obscene and revoked or denied the second-class mailing permit for sixty-two publications.[9] The banned magazines included *Spark, Stocking Parade, Peek, Real Romance, Front Page Detective, Judge, Argosy,* and the ever-maligned *Police Gazette.*[10] Although Walker would be a formidable *Esquire* foe, Arnold Gingrich was never sure why he went after *Esquire* with such zeal. "We were never able to find out whether his animus in the Esquire Post Office Case was political or religious. In either case it went very deep."[11]

The case against *Esquire* was not the first post office attempt at censorship. The history of that department's attempts to regulate publications goes back to 1836 and President Andrew Jackson. That was the year Congress first considered regulating mail to keep Abolitionist broadsheets—Jackson called them "incendiaries"—from being delivered in the South where, the president said, the publications were likely to stir up bitterness and violence. When Jackson asked Congress to pass a law instructing postmasters to destroy the writings, Congress refused. In 1865 Congress again considered the problem of obscenity in the mails, and a bill was passed authorizing postmasters to seize obscene mail if the seal of the envelope did not have to be broken. The new law allowed the post office to criminally prosecute anyone who disseminated such material. That would include most magazines, which, like *Esquire,* were not shipped in sealed envelopes. All of this, however, was simply prologue for the 1873 arrival in Washington of twenty-eight-year-old Anthony Comstock, the lobbyist for the Committee for the Suppression of Vice, sponsored by the New York YMCA.

Comstock began his crusading as a vice vigilante some years before he came to Washington. He became so obsessed with the idea of obscenity that he took time off from his job as a clerk in a Brooklyn dry goods store to track down and seize what he believed to be pornographic literature. "I have seized and destroyed more than five tons [of] obscene books and pamphlets," he told one congressman. As a result of his actions, fifty dealers were arrested and six publishers died after Comstock labeled them pornographers. One committed suicide. Comstock also looked for obscenity in advertisements in lowbrow magazines like *New Varieties* and *Illustrated Police Gazette*. Comstock would send for the material advertised and, if he thought it obscene, would turn it over to a federal marshal. He worked with law enforcement officials to have people like the sisters Victoria Woodhull and Tennessee Claflin arrested for advocating women's rights and free love in their publication, *Woodhull and Claflin's Weekly*. It was the material in the *Weekly* that drove Comstock to Washington to push for legislation that would ban obscenity from the mail.[12] The Comstock Act, as it came to be called, was passed in 1874 and specified that no obscene, lewd, or lascivious publication should be carried in the mail, and anyone who knowingly mailed or received these obscene items should be sent to jail for as much as ten years. The bill passed unanimously in the Senate, and only thirty representatives voted against it in the House. After the bill became law, Comstock was made a special agent of the Post Office Department.

Five years after the Comstock Act was passed, Congress enacted a seemingly unrelated piece of legislation, the Postal Act of March 3, 1879, which established the lower, second-class mailing rates for publications. As a result, the number of magazines rose from 700 in 1865 to 3,300 in 1985.[13] The new postal act actually added to the censorship power of the post office, however, giving it not only the right of criminal prosecution but also the right to rescind cheap mailing rates to punish publishers of what the post office considered obscene. The post office also banned books it considered obscene. Banned from the mails were, among many other volumes, *The Sex*

Side of Life: An Explanation for Young People, by Marie Ware Dennett, one of the founders of the Planned Parenthood League; *Rasputin, the Holy Devil,* a biography, by Rene Fulop-Miller; *Lady Chatterley's Lover,* by D. H. Lawrence; *The Gods Are Athirst,* by Anatole France; *Lysistrata,* by Aristophanes; and *Ulysses,* by James Joyce. Also banned were a reproduction of Michelangelo's Sistine Chapel frescos and some rare Chinese paintings mailed to the Field Museum in Chicago.[14]

In 1933, in a case involving the alleged obscenity of James Joyce's *Ulysses,* things began to change. A copy of Joyce's book was brought into the United States by an actress and confiscated by customs agents in New York. Just as the post office had the authority to determine what was obscene in the mails, the customs service had the power to decide what was obscene and confiscate it. They took *Ulysses,* and that touched off a suit brought by Random House, the New York publisher who was preparing an American printing of the novel. In essence, the attorneys for the publisher asked the federal district court to consider the book as a whole, not just isolated passages. Federal Judge John Woolsey agreed with Random House. Despite the novel's frankness, Judge Woolsey said, he felt Joyce was sincerely motivated in his attempt to depict a slice of life in Dublin. "When such a real artist in words, as Joyce undoubtedly is, seeks to draw a true picture of the lower class in a European city, ought it to be impossible for the American public to legally see that picture?"[15] The case was appealed, but Woolsey was upheld. Essentially, the ruling meant that immature or susceptible people could not be the measuring stick for a book's obscenity; any promotion of lust must occur in normal adults.

The ruling also said that any harm must come from reading the whole work and not selected passages, and that special consideration must be made for a book's literary, scientific, or educational value. In 1940 another ruling, this time involving magazines, upheld the new standards of the Woolsey decision. A Washington, D.C., bookseller named Parmelee tried to import six copies of a European magazine, *Nudism in Modern Life.* In addition to writing, the book contained twenty-three unretouched photographs of nudists. On appeal, Parmelee won his case and the ruling by Judge Learned Hand established the idea that community standards could determine obscenity.

All of this was the background for the post office action against *Esquire*. After the Parmelee case, there was a new definition of censorship in the federal courts, but not in the post office. The attempt to lift the second-class permit for *Esquire* came as no surprise to people who followed the pronouncements of Postmaster General Walker. In the post office's *Annual Report* of 1942 Walker said that a second-class mailing permit was a "privilege" that was a "certificate of good moral character," and he suggested that he had the power to deny the permit even when the magazine had published nothing that was actually nonmailable. "Some criticism [of our new policies] is expected," Walker wrote.[16]

The *Esquire* hearing before three assistant postmasters appointed by Walker began on October 19, 1943. Gingrich initially rented a room at the Statler Hotel in Washington to use as *Esquire*'s headquarters during the hearing. As the seriousness of the case became apparent, he expanded his quarters until the magazine occupied almost an entire floor of the hotel. *Esquire*'s attorney was Bruce Bromley of the New York firm of Cravath, de Gersdorff, Swaine and Wood. His assistant was another lawyer in that firm, Jack Harding, who, along with Gingrich, worked at getting witnesses to testify for *Esquire*, investigating post office witnesses, and making sure witnesses stayed to testify when the trial was delayed.[17] The post office was represented by Calvin Hassell, a lawyer who was a Boy Scout volunteer and former postman.[18]

In order to qualify for second-class mailing, a magazine had to (and must still) meet four criteria: it must be issued regularly at least four times a year with a date of issue, from a fixed office of publication, in a printed form with paper covers, and "it must be originated and published for the dissemination of information of a public character, or devoted to literature, the sciences, arts or some special industry, and having a legitimate list of subscribers."[19] It was this last provision that the post office would use in an attempt to revoke *Esquire*'s permit.

Of the ninety items cited by the post office as obscene in the magazine, twenty-two were Varga Girl illustrations. There were also cartoons, photographs, and other illustrations. Literary items cited included a short story by Paul Gallico, excerpts from military base newspapers, a parody of "The Night Before Christmas," and a review

of a Broadway show, *Star and Garter*. The words considered obscene
by the post office included *bottom, juke, diddle, bawdy house, prostitute, street-walker, syphilis, sunny south* (referring to a woman's
posterior), *fanny*, and *sonofabitch*. One cartoon cited as obscene
showed a group of soldiers surrounded by women with spears. Underneath the picture is written, "It's no use Sarge, we are outnumbered. Yippee!" In another, two air raid wardens are on a roof looking
through a transom. The light has come on, revealing an artist's studio where there is a nude model, and one man says, "To think I gave
up drawing." One of the military base jokes reproduced in *Esquire*
was: A woman says, "Would you like to see where I was operated on?"
And the man says, "No, I hate hospitals."[20]

The hearing began on October 19, 1943, and lasted until November 6. Transcripts fill three volumes and more than eighteen hundred pages. Perhaps the best-known witness for the defense was H. L.
Mencken, the editor of *The American Mercury*. The most famous
post office witness was the Reverend Peter Marshall, minister of the
New York Avenue Presbyterian Church in Washington, D.C., a future chaplain of the U.S. Senate and a prominent religious broadcaster. Mencken, who was also the author of *The American
Language*, testified about the obscenity of words found in *Esquire*:

> "Sunny south" is obviously an attempt at humor. I myself in such a situation use the word "caboose," but then
> everybody has his favorites,. You have to, sometime in this
> life, living a biological life of mammals, refer to backside,
> and in humorous writing, which this is, there is an effort
> to invent charming and, if possible, euphemous backsides. . . . The idea that it was obscene shocks me. . . . It
> seems to be a term of limited situation . . . what he would
> call it if she were facing south, I don't know. . . . I had a
> note about "backside," which is considered much more—
> "behind" was taught to me as a boy in the nursery as a
> children's euphemism. I knew no other word for the rear
> part until I was probably four years of age and became
> sophisticated. At the age of three all children in Baltimore
> in the kind of society I was brought up with called "backside" the backside and it wasn't considered unpleasant or

indecent. They knew no other word, and there was nothing obscene about it at that age. That is before Freud.
Children didn't know anything about sex.[21]

Peter Marshall didn't seem to have as much fun as Mencken, and
he certainly didn't agree with him:

> My impression of the policy, editorial policy and tone
> of the magazine is that it tends to make that which is im-
> moral modern, sophisticated, and commonplace, to sug-
> gest that fornication and adultery, pre-marital relations,
> extra-marital relations, are the conventional conduct of the
> American people to which I, as a minister, must protest,
> knowing it to be not so and believing it to be definitely
> injurious to public morals and particularly to the readers
> of this magazine. . . . I would like to mention . . . this par-
> ticular reference.

>> "Here lies the body
>> Of poor old Charlotte.
>> Born a virgin,
>> Died a harlot.
>> For eighteen years she kept her virginity,
>> An all-time record in this vicinity."

> That, it seems to me, expresses the very thing that I find
> most objectionable in the editorial tone and policy of the
> magazine, a suggestion that there is anything unusual in
> virginity until eighteen years of age. . . . I believe that
> womanhood has definitely been lowered by the achieve-
> ment of equality with men. . . . The whole tendency of this
> magazine, it seems to me, is to degrade and lower [the]
> moral tone.[22]

Arnold Gingrich testified as the spokesman for *Esquire* and was
on the stand for more than a week. He was repetitive, dull, and ver-
bose. In more than four hundred pages (pages 973–1414) in the
official record he gives a personal biography, history of the magazine,

background on major contributors, analysis of how cartoons are chosen, and feature-by-feature critique of each issue of *Esquire* in question. He also talks about the protracted negotiations with the post office over content and about the magazine as a morale booster for American troops. "My testimony . . . was not long-winded just because I wanted it to be," Gingrich wrote in his memoirs, "but at least in part because Bromley ordered me onto the stand to engage in what was a tactic tantamount to filibustering. Bromley wanted to gain some time . . . and asked me if I thought I could get in there and just stall and 'hold up the game for a couple of days.' . . . Whatever his reason was for wanting to gain time now and then, he would simply send me back in there. . . . Whenever this happened, I would talk so long and fast that the hearing room stenographer would shrug at her stenotype." Gingrich, and not David Smart, *Esquire*'s publisher, was chosen to testify because "[Bromley] feared Dave's low boiling point if he should happen to be asked a question that he considered stupid."[23]

But it was not Gingrich's long-winded testimony, Mencken's wit, or Peter Marshall's impassioned oratory that captured the imagination of the press during the hearing. It was the famous *Esquire* pinup, the Varga Girl, *Time* magazine wrote in its coverage of the trial:

> Boston [Harvard] Psychiatrist Kenneth Tillotson gazed soberly at samples of Artist Alberto Vargas's skimpily clad babes, then testified, "as a doctor who has examined hundreds of women." Said he: Varga girls are "inspiring" and not abnormally hippy, though sometimes their feet are too big. . . . Testified Yale Psychiatrist Clements Fry: "I have seen Varga girls pasted up in boys' rooms at Yale, and don't think the boys pay a great deal of attention to them."[24]

For all the problems the case may have caused *Esquire*, it also brought reams of publicity, most of it centered around the Varga Girl. Newspapers that normally wouldn't have printed pinups reproduced pictures of the *Esquire* drawings. Anticipating the possibility that the magazine might lose its mailing rights, Vargas prepared a special painting of a girl in a Victorian hoopskirt and bonnet.[25] It was never published.

In closing arguments, the post office's Hassell hammered away at the theme of obscenity in *Esquire*:

> Here we have in this publication these gatefolds, as they are called, two-page size, color pictures of what has been referred to here as the "glorification of American womanhood." I do not accept that description of it. It does not describe these pictures at all. The fact that young soldiers do pin them up in their barracks means, and it is a very clear indication to me, that they get some sexual enjoyment from viewing them.
>
> I submit to this Board that the publication *Esquire* has been a trail-blazer in pandering to the prurient ever since it was established, and thus far it is not equalled by any other publication enjoying this high privilege, this subsidy from the American people.
>
> In all this testimony we have heard here . . . I feel that counsel has sought to accustom all of us to these Varga wenches and the other objectionable material in this publication. . . . But I want this Board to please bear in mind . . . the fact that the Board is here . . . to determine . . . one question only: whether this publication is entitled to continue to enjoy the prestige and stamp of approval of the Post Office Department; whether it is entitled to a subsidy from the hard-pressed taxpayer of over half a million dollars a year; whether it is designed for the "public good" as an "efficient educator" and as a "disseminator of useful knowledge."[26]

Bromley answered in more reasoned, less passionate rhetoric:

> It seems to me . . . Mr. Hassell is trying to induce you . . . to define information of a public character as being useful, helpful, beneficial information. I think material which entertains is information of a public character, just as much as the current news items carried in a magazine like *Time*.

Under the words of the statute, under the obvious intent which Congress must have had, magazines like *Cos-
mopolitan*, *Red Book*, while largely devoted to fiction,
constantly contain articles that are just entertaining, that
are not useful, they don't educate anybody, but they give
pleasure in reading. It was never the intention of Congress,
looking at all the words they used . . . to say that only a
magazine like *Time* is intended to second-class privileges.

At no time within [*Esquire*'s] ten-year history . . . has
this magazine ever been prosecuted by any public authority anywhere for obscenity or indecency. . . . And if there
is anything to the argument that this magazine of sophistication constitutes a threat to our form of government or
to morals, don't you think the Solicitor could have found
out of this great city in which must reside thousands of
men of knowledge, experience, distinction, and ability,
some one or two who could have come here and told us
about it?[27]

On November 14, the Postal Board voted two to one in favor of
allowing *Esquire* to keep its second-class mailing privileges. The cel-
ebration in the magazine's Chicago offices was not a long one, however. Six weeks later, on December 30, Postmaster General Walker
overruled his hearing board and denied *Esquire* its second-class permit. He said,

The plain language of this [second-class permit] does
not assume that a publication must in fact be "obscene"
within the intendment of the postal obscenity statutes before it can be found not to be "originated and published
for the dissemination of information of a public character, or devoted to literature, the sciences, arts, or some special interest." . . . I am unable to conclude that . . .
Congress did intend or now intends that this publication
be entitled to enjoy the second class mailing privileges . . .
and permit it to receive at the hands of the government a
preference in post charges of approximately $500,000 per
annum.[28]

Bromley called Walker's decision "a far-reaching, arbitrary, capricious decision by which one man sets himself up to decide what is in the public welfare." Gingrich hinted that the postmaster general was following the dictates of the Catholic Church: "He possibly had a commitment to carry out somebody else's wishes." The editor was probably remembering the boycott imposed by the Catholic Church in the days when *Ken* was under fire from the pulpit. But Catholic Bishop John Francis Noll of Fort Wayne, Indiana, chairman of the National Organization for Decent Literature, said, "[Esquire's] not even on our disapproved list for a year . . . as far as I know he [Walker] doesn't think of me in connection with this *Esquire* business."[29]

Six weeks later, on February 15, *Esquire* took the case, now called *Walker v. Esquire*, from the post office hearing room to U.S. district court. But the trial in the courtroom would be different from the postal hearings. Both parties agreed in a pretrial conference that the suit would not involve federal obscenity statutes but would instead be tried to determine whether *Esquire* met the conditions for second-class mailing. The two sides also agreed that *Esquire* could continue to receive second-class mailing privileges until the matter was settled in court. If *Esquire* lost, it would pay the difference between second-class and first-class rates to the government. From the beginning, when the judge for the case was announced, it seemed the magazine would have a tough time.

T. Whitfield Davidson of Ennis, Texas, was sitting temporarily as a district judge in the District of Columbia. Appointed to the federal bench in 1936 by Franklin Roosevelt, Davidson was an American classic. He was born in a log cabin in the East Texas hills and studied history, law, and the Bible by firelight while he made a living splitting rails. With almost no formal education, he was admitted to the bar in 1903, became city attorney of Marshall, Texas, in 1907 and was elected to the state senate in 1920. Davidson was elected lieutenant governor in 1922 and made an unsuccessful race for governor two years later. Although he expressed fears over what he called "the amalgamation of the races," Davidson had a reputation as an enemy of the Ku Klux Klan.[30] Now this sixty-eight-year-old Texan would decide on the fitness of a sophisticated men's magazine to receive what the post office was calling a federal subsidy for mailing. Bromley defended *Esquire*'s merit and introduced other magazines with second-class permits—*Hobo News, Gag, Laff, Love, Hit,* and *Army and Navy Parade*—to show that periodicals with far less literary and artistic content still were allowed lower mailing rates. Bernard Deinard, the attorney for the post office, made his point by waving a copy of *Esquire* before the judge and shouting, "Is this what Congress granted a bounty for?"[31]

On July 27 Judge Davidson ruled, "The Postmaster General's determination that *Esquire* was not originated and published for the dissemination of information of a public character, or devoted to literature, the sciences, arts or some special industry, was not clearly wrong nor unlawfully made, nor arbitrary, capricious or unsupported by substantial evidence."[32] The judge also delved into the minds of the congressmen who had voted for the second-class permit legislation in the 1870s, saying they were brought up on *McGuffey's Reader* and that was the standard by which they judged the educational value of magazines. Judge Davidson said free speech and obscenity were not a part of the case.[33] In his memoirs, Gingrich wrote, "In contrast to [Judge Davidson] the postmaster general himself began to seem almost libertarian. . . . It was hard to conceive of a twentieth-century magazine that might have measured either down or up to [*McGuffey's Reader*], the direction depending on one's point of view."[34] Naturally, *Esquire* appealed the decision.

The appeal was heard by Judge Thurman Arnold of the U.S. Court of Appeals in Washington, D.C., who rendered his judgment on June 4, 1945, almost a year after the district court ruling. In this third round of the *Esquire* battle, the magazine won. Judge Arnold ruled that Congress never intended for the postmaster general to act as a censor or arbiter of good taste. It is inconceivable, Judge Arnold wrote, that Congress delegated to postal officials such broad power over publications, "the power first to determine what is good for the public to read and then to force compliance." And, he added:

> We intend no criticism of counsel for the Post Office. They were faced with an impossible task. They undertook it with sincerity. But their very sincerity makes the record useful as a memorial to commemorate the utter confusion and lack of intelligible standards which can never be escaped when that task is attempted. We believe that the

> Post Office officials should experience a feeling of relief
> if they are limited to the more prosaic function of seeing
> to it that "neither snow nor rain nor heat nor gloom of
> night stays these couriers from the swift completion of
> their appointed rounds."[35]

This time it was the post office's turn to appeal.

When the *Esquire* case went before the U.S. Supreme Court, it was with a different name. Frank Walker resigned as postmaster general on June 30, 1945, less than two months after the death of Franklin Roosevelt. His successor, appointed by Harry Truman, was Robert E. Hannegan, the chairman of the Democratic National Committee and commissioner of Internal Revenue. Hannegan was a former member of the St. Louis political machine; he had changed his allegiance in the middle of the 1936 Senate campaign and supported Truman rather than his opponent, Governor Lloyd C. Stark. Truman won, carrying St. Louis, and when Walker resigned, Truman remembered his old friend Hannegan, who had also been the first person to tell Truman he was Roosevelt's choice for vice-president.[36] The case was now called *Hannegan v. Esquire* and was argued before the Supreme Court in the October 1945 term.

By now the briefs had a familiar ring. Culled from the arguments were the patriotism theme *Esquire*'s attorneys had used before the postal board and the thundering moral indignation the post office lawyers had evoked before the district court. The question before the Supreme Court was simply whether or not the postmaster general had the power to decide what magazines were deserving of second class permits. On February 4, 1946, Justice William O. Douglas, writing for a unanimous court, ruled,

> The policy of Congress had been clear. It has been to
> encourage the distribution of periodicals . . . because it
> thought that these publications as a class contributed to
> the public good. The standards have been criticized, but
> not on the ground that they provide for censorship. . . .
> The provisions [of the second-class mailing act] would
> have to be far more explicit for us to assume that Congress made such a radical departure from our traditions

[of free speech] and undertook to clothe the Postmaster General with the power to supervise the tastes of the reading public of the country.

It is plain, as we have said, that the favorable second-class permits were granted periodicals meeting the requirements of [the law] so that the public good might be served through a dissemination of the class of periodicals described. But that is a far cry from assuming that Congress had any idea that each applicant for the second-class rate must convince the Postmaster General that his publication positively contributes to the public good or public welfare. Under our system of government there is an accommodation for the widest varieties of tastes and ideas. . . . The power to determine whether a periodical which is mailable contains information of a public character . . . does not include the further power to determine whether the contents meet with some standard of the public good or welfare.[37]

After three years of legal battles, *Esquire* was assured of the right to second-class mailing rates. On the surface, the *Esquire* trial was about censorship and the Varga Girl. But there is a deeper meaning to those years in court. The trial was also about rural versus urban sensibilities, about the dominance of old-time Christianity, and about changing sexual mores in America. Look at *Esquire*'s opponents. Frank Walker, the postmaster general, was from Montana, hardly an urban state, but he later developed ties to the eastern moneyed establishment through his uncle's theater chain. He graduated from law school at Notre Dame and was a prominent Catholic layman. T. Whitfield Davidson, the U.S. district court judge who issued the initial court ruling in the *Esquire* case, was from Ennis, Texas, prided himself on studying the Bible by firelight, and believed in segregation, which was not uncommon at the time. Both were children of the nineteenth century, and both shared the world view of Anthony Comstock, whose censorship campaign was church-related.

Esquire represented a new set of values forged in urban America by men who had adopted the post–World War I ethos of sexual permissiveness. Smart and Gingrich used frankly sexual literature and illustrations that violated the Victorian worldview of Walker and Davidson. The new sexuality exemplified by the flapper and, more specifically, the Varga Girl, was what rankled Peter Marshall, who represented traditional mainstream Christian thought. It was also what amused H. L. Mencken, the great iconoclast of the early twentieth century who ridiculed American mainstream thought in the *American Mercury* as "the hallucinations of Rotary, the Gideons, the D. A. R., the American Legion, the League of American Penwomen, the Methodist Board of Temperance, Prohibition, public morals, and a multitude of other such klans and sodalities."[38] In the eyes of *Esquire*'s opponents, the magazine truly was "unholy" as Henry Pringle had written a decade earlier in *Scribner's*. After all, wasn't this the magazine that said in its 1936 promotional literature that its ideal reader "hadn't been to church since the last time he ushered at a wedding?"[39]

When the U.S. Post Office first tried to censor *Esquire* in 1940, the magazine stood alone among mainstream periodicals as an advocate of the new sexuality. Hollywood's movies, which were largely written and directed by men from America's small towns, were subject to the self-censorship of the Motion Picture Production Code, which required that films show "the correct standards of life."[40] Popular magazines like *The Saturday Evening Post* interpreted America as being a land of small towns characterized by conservative, middle-class complacency and where the Norman Rockwell illustrations represented reality, not wishful thinking. Radio networks kept their programming wholesome to avoid alienating potential buyers of sponsors' products. In most popular culture, then, America was still living in the small towns that had dominated the country before the urban explosion of the 1920s. The *Esquire* ruling helped shatter the calm façade that was already cracking in the Hollywood *film noir* "B" movies. The Court's decision gave the final push into reality to a country whose popular culture still tucked its sexuality into twin beds with the lights out.

The *Esquire* victory in the U.S. Supreme Court was a hollow one for Arnold Gingrich. By 1946, when the ruling was issued, he had left the magazine, cashed in his pension, and moved to Switzerland. Gingrich had resigned as editor at the end of July the year before the ruling was issued. On paper, he was European editor, but in fact his duties at the magazine had ended. He was forty years old when he resigned. Actually, Gingrich had seen his power as editor ebbing away since the magazine became a vehicle for pinups in 1940. He had suggested from time to time that if Smart was going to dictate editorial policy, he should be both editor and publisher, but Smart only took both titles after Gingrich resigned.[41] Gingrich says in his memoirs that he "retired," but it is apparent that it was frustration with Smart that drove him away. *Esquire* was, after all, his brainchild; he had made it a vehicle for good, unconventional writing, discovered the cartoonists, decided on Esky as a corporate symbol, picked George Petty to draw pinups, and begun the extensive coverage of jazz. But no matter what decision he made, there was David Smart, looking over his shoulder, often demanding changes.[42]

Gingrich was constantly overruled by Smart, who wanted more cartoons and more pinups at the expense of the element Gingrich felt was essential—literary quality. The magazine was no longer the mixture of popular and serious culture Gingrich had started. Add to that the exhaustion that came from editing three magazines—*Esquire*, *Ken*, and *Coronet*—at the same time, and it's no wonder he left. It was more than just a decision to leave a job; it was like the breakup of a marriage.[43] These two men were the original odd couple—one literary and erudite, the other crass and mercurial. Gingrich allowed Smart to pick out his house for him, decide where his country estate would be and where he would go on vacation. Smart, of course, continued to publish the magazine without Gingrich, but it was never the same again. Without its founding editor, *Esquire* was, as Oscar Dystel said, "a magazine without a soul."[44] It would not regain its bearings again until Gingrich returned.

Esquire's court battles didn't end with the settlement of the post office case. Soon, the magazine was faced with a lawsuit by Alberto Vargas, who wanted his name back, and another by a jazz writer from the pages of *Esquire*.

On May 23, 1944, Alberto Vargas signed a new contract with *Esquire*. Vargas thought "Uncle David" was giving him a raise. Actually, through Smart's legal maneuvering, the artist would be making less money. First, the new contract specified that he was no longer an *Esquire* employee but was instead an independent contractor. Second, it required Vargas to supply *Esquire* with a painting a week for the next ten years. The contract also denied Vargas the right to do outside work. His pay was to be eighteen thousand dollars for each eighteen-month period, or one thousand dollars a month. With no outside income from advertising accounts and no additional money for calendar sales, Vargas was making less money for more work.[45]

Vargas never questioned "Uncle David." He signed the contract and never even looked at it until a year later. After he finally read it and realized what he had signed, Vargas went to Smart and told him a painting a week was an impossibility and then started discussing salary. Smart threw Vargas out of his office. Four days later, there was a second meeting with the artist and his wife, and Smart threatened to see that Vargas never worked again in the United States. His wife, Anna Mae, answered, "In that case, Mr. Smart, all we have is our courage and each other. We have no fear when we have that."[46]

Smart ordered Vargas's signature pulled from the last two of his paintings the magazine ran in 1947. They were called *Esquire* Girls, and the artist was not named. On April 30, 1946, the artist filed suit against Esquire, Inc. in Illinois District Court. Less than a month later, Judge Michael L. Igoe ruled in favor of Vargas. But *Esquire* appealed, and on February 27, 1948, the Illinois Circuit Court of Appeals reversed the original decision. Varga was nothing more than a trademark held by a corporation, and Alberto Vargas could never again work under the name he had made famous.

Meanwhile, without Gingrich, Smart tried to continue the famous *Esquire* jazz poll. He hired Ernest Anderson to write the feature, a decision that caused outrage in modern jazz circles. Anderson was a publicist for Eddie Condon, a jazz guitarist, banjo player, and vocalist who was closely associated with post–New Orleans white musicians. Even though he had recorded with Louis Armstrong and Fats Waller, Condon was better known for his work with Bix Beiderbecke, a white jazz trumpeter from Davenport, Iowa. Under Smart and Anderson, the amount of space devoted to the jazz poll was reduced and the annual *Esquire Jazz Book* featured thirty-seven photos of white musicians and only seventeen of black instrumentalists and singers. It was as if Anderson were still doing publicity for Condon, who had opened a jazz club in New York in 1945.

"If the attempt to capture the book for Condon and his friends had not been so blatantly opportunistic, perhaps the uproar that ensued might have been avoided," Leonard Feather wrote, "but the tone and intent of the book left room for no reaction but anger on the part of the musicians who had been given short shrift."[47] Equally outraged was the *Amsterdam News*, New York's leading African American newspaper, which complained, "There is a series of about twenty pictures of the Condon group in an eight-page spread and not a single Negro face appears among them. It reeks of 'Dixieland' and 'white supremacy' music."[48]

As a result, a group of thirty-three jazz musicians who were previous *Esquire* award winners wrote to Smart, protesting the poll and its domination by Condon and Dixieland music. They said the results were an insult and announced they would not take part in future *Esquire* polls. The letter was signed by Louis Armstrong, Coleman Hawkins, Roy Eldridge, Red Norvo, Buddy Rich, Charlie Shavers, Dizzy Gillespie, Willie Smith, Boyd Raeburn, Charlie Ventura, Miles Davis, Al Casey, Flip Phillips, Pete Candoli, Shadow Wilson, Trummy Young, Tad Dameron, Sarah Vaughn, Aaron Sachs, Billie Holiday, Buck Clayton, Big Sid Catlett, Johnny Hodges, Harry Carney, Oscar Pettiford, Cootie Williams, Teddy Wilson, Ella Fitzgerald, Duke Ellington, Ray Nance, Nat "King" Cole, Chubby Jackson, and J. C. Heard.[49] After the letter was sent, eighteen of the twenty jazz experts associated with the *Esquire* poll resigned. Robert Goffin, the Belgian jazz writer who, with Gingrich, had started the *Esquire* jazz poll, sued the magazine because he was not allowed to take part in the 1947 article. The case was settled out of court, but part of Goffin's settlement was said to be a promise from Smart that *Esquire* would never run a jazz poll again.[50] And it never did.

Battered by lawsuits, suffering from the loss of Gingrich and Vargas, and stung by the end of the jazz poll, *Esquire* limped into postwar America. The magazine had won the right to the name *Varga*, but there was no artist to draw the pinups; it had the U.S. Supreme Court's decision guaranteeing it second-class mailing privileges, but its circulation was now mostly among men forty and older. The formula of Varga Girls, spicy jokes, and racy cartoons began to have less relevance as Americans began searching for a new life away from Jeeps and olive drab. *Esquire*'s favorable court decisions were a hollow victory—it had won the right to publish a magazine the public apparently no longer found interesting. But the formula it had created opened the way for an even bigger publishing sensation, whose bow-tied rabbit replaced the popeyed Esky as a symbol of male sophistication.

8 Esky's Metamorphosis

O n the cover of the June 1946 *Esquire* there is a cartoon of a bride and groom being escorted into a one-room shanty made of scraps of lumber and covered with what appears to be used shingling. The shanty is in the green outskirts of town, beyond the skyline that appears in the background. Friends and relatives, dressed in top hats and expensive gowns, applaud as the groom prepares to take the bride across the threshold of the shack. Esky watches this strange ceremony from a swing attached to the magazine's nameplate. He is above the scene, like some angel from another time, looking down to see how these mortals have changed since his days on earth.

Welcome home, soldier. You've got the real thing now, not just a paper doll. And the reality of the postwar years of housing shortages, peaking automobile sales, exploding birth rates, suburban development, atomic paranoia, and finding new jobs was hardly the stuff of a girlie magazine. The old camp humor seemed boring now, and the pinups had lost some of their allure. "This Is the Army, Mr. Jones," the Andrews Sisters sang during the forty-five months of combat when *Esquire* was called a morale builder. But this postwar world was more like the Bob Dylan song that came some twenty years later—"Something's happening and you don't know what it is, do you, Mister Jones?"

Actually, no one knew what was happening. During the war years, when people thought about what the world would be like after the fighting was over, they imagined an America with 1929 post-crash values and the economy of the early 1920s. It would be the same as life before the Depression, only changed a little by a hangover from wartime controls.[1] It was not to be a return to the future, however. The post–World War II era was altogether different from either the boom of the 1920s or the Depression and war that followed. It wasn't only Mr. Jones who wondered what it was. Of course, the postwar world involved consumerism—the pent-up wants from the years of wearing only khaki and blue were unleashed on a nation of business-men who couldn't make toasters, cars, jewelry, power lawn mowers, dishwashers, washing machines, civilian clothes, and tract housing fast enough. This new world filled with new brides and new babies also brought an unprecedented emphasis on The Family and The Home. The den, the one room in the house that was traditionally male-dominated, became the family room. In its idealized form, the home would contain sexual enjoyment, material comfort, well-ad-justed children, and evidence of personal success for husbands and wives who performed well their clearly defined roles.[2] How was a magazine like *Esquire* that emphasized rakish behavior and showgirls supposed to exist in an era when do-it-yourself home repair was more important to American males than fantasies of Miss January? David Smart, now both editor and publisher, coped. He left the basic *Esquire* formula intact and believed his magazine would survive the postwar rush to domesticity. *Esquire* continued to sell, but older men were buying it, using it to rekindle a nostalgia for their youth. Younger men were buying ranches and split levels, and any thoughts of chorus girls were sublimated to real worries about playpens and lawns.

After Gingrich left, Smart hired Frederick Birmingham as man-aging editor of *Esquire*. Birmingham (1911–1982) was the son of John Francis and Louise Westher Birmingham, who ran a diner—Birmingham always called it a one-arm joint—on New York's East Side. He was an unexpected child—his mother was forty-eight when he was born. Like Arnold Gingrich, Birmingham showed an early interest in music, but there was an important difference between the two men. As a musician, Birmingham was talented; Gingrich wasn't. In fact, Birmingham was a talented enough pianist to win musical scholarships in New York and, later, to Trinity School. By the time he was twelve, he had played in Carnegie Hall and sung with the choir of the Church of Saint John the Divine in New York. In high school at Trinity, his musical career ended. One Sunday afternoon he went mountain climbing, took a bad step, and slid down a cliff, avoiding death only by grabbing the branch of a tree. He held onto it for six hours until help came, but it was a cold day, and by the time he was rescued, his hands were frozen. Initially, doctors treating him decided to amputate his hands, but Birmingham insisted on being taken to a family doctor, who saved his hands and treated him for months when he had no feeling in his fingers. To restore his feeling, the doctor brought Birmingham a typewriter, and that is when he started writing.[3]

After graduating from Trinity, Birmingham attended Dartmouth College, where he received a B.A. in 1933. Before becoming managing editor of *Esquire* he had an itinerant career in journalism. In 1935 he was eastern editor for *Esquire*'s trade magazine, *Apparel Arts*. Although he continued at that magazine as a consulting editor until 1941, the year he married Frances Atherton, he went to work full-time for *Time* in 1936. Between 1937 and 1939 he wrote a cartoon-essay feature for the Bell Syndicate and for the North American Newspaper Alliance, and was an editor for Ogden-Whitney, a New York publishing house. In 1939 he went to work in the New York sales promotion office of *Esquire* as a copywriter and sales promotions manager. During World War II, Birmingham became a senior editor in the Office of Wartime Information, then transferred to the navy, where he became a lieutenant commander. When the war ended, he returned to *Esquire* as managing editor.

In his new position, Birmingham constantly feared for his job. He was afraid to take vacations because leaving for a week or two might mean someone else would be sitting at his desk when he returned.[4] He was also deferential to Smart, who constantly came up with unworkable ideas for the postwar *Esquire*. One month, for example, Smart would decide all of *Esquire*'s fiction would be mysteries. The next month, he would decree that it would all be westerns. "Fred had a ten-gallon hat and spurs on his desk, to let everyone see that westerns were now the thing and that any story that wasn't a western just wasn't an *Esquire* story," Arnold Gingrich wrote in his memoirs.[5] Birmingham was, in other words, a yes man, but with Smart and his mercurial personality, it was hard to know from day to day what editorial policy you were supporting. Abe Blinder, *Esquire*'s circulation manager, remembers Birmingham as "superficially talented."[6] Oscar Dystel, the editor of *Coronet*, thinks of Birmingham as facile. "He was a fast-thinking Wasp-type, and David was attracted to that,"

Dystel said. "He was a nonfiction editor and he was a kind of supplicant to David Smart to a point where it annoyed me. . . . he was really just a journeyman editor, trying to carry the flame that was started by Arnold."[7] Birmingham was a huge man, six foot five, and it was often comical to see him kowtowing to Smart, who was only five six. It was also during his tenure as managing editor that Birmingham began drinking heavily, often having three brandy Alexanders with lunch.[8]

Birmingham had a lot of problems that never plagued Arnold Gingrich. After the war, *Esquire*'s circulation began to slip as paper rationing ended and other magazines returned to their prewar size. Much of *Esquire*'s circulation during World War II had come from people who bought the magazine instead of their favorite periodical, which might have been unavailable because of wartime shortages. Paper shortages and rationing cut down on the size of most magazines, unless they, like *Esquire*, printed on cheaper paper, and the skimpy size made them unappealing. When the war ended, these marginal readers dropped *Esquire* and returned to their first choices.[9] The end of the war and the Supreme Court's favorable ruling also added another new element—competition. As long as there was a paper shortage or a court threat, it was unlikely a new magazine would begin using the *Esquire* formula of girls, cartoons, and daring fiction. Once the war ended, however, competition flourished. Before the war only one periodical, *For Men*, published in the mid-thirties by Fawcett, attempted to capture part of the *Esquire* market. After the war, the competition grew, but most of the *Esquire* rivals—*Night and Day, Wink, Brief, Paris Life, Keyhole, Titter, Eye, Pepper, Candid Whirl, Cover Girl Models, Scope, Picture Fun, Flirt, Eyeful,* and *Beauty Parade*—ignored quality and sold sex and cartoons. It was a kind of sex alien to *Esquire* readers. As Theodore Peterson writes,

> In the forties and fifties . . . many of the magazines looked as if their editors had pored over the works of Freud, Krafft-Ebing, and Wilhelm Stekel. Sadism, masochism, fetishism, perversions, all were implicit in the prose and pictures of a covey of magazines. . . . When [models] posed in the nude or its approximation, it was

not always with simple seductiveness. She wore stilt heels or let her long hair drape down her body; she was enmeshed in chains or covered with gilt and powdered glass which, the caption pointed out, could "cut into the skin." She wrestled lion cubs and vicious dogs. She was shown being flogged, being frozen in a cake of ice, being shot from a cannon.[10]

What had *Esquire* wrought? Actually, this change in the girlie market came more from Hollywood than from *Esquire*. The 1940s were the decade of *film noir*, that genre that made the wholesome women of the war years over into *femmes fatales*. Hollywood's women died at the end of their evil adventures; the women featured in photographs in the new girlie magazines were tortured much as the women shown in paintings on the covers of pulp magazines two decades earlier had been. Although *Esquire* was not responsible for this change in attitude and did little to promote it, the *femme fatale* crept into its pages and, occasionally, stood beside the curvaceous *Esquire* girl. In April 1948 an article by Harry Sperber appeared with the title "The Fraulein Wins the Peace." The subhead proclaimed, "Homesick G.I.s are easy prey for German girls whose favors furnish a sugar coating for Nazi propaganda." In a year when the cold war was beginning and memories of Hitler were fresh, a *femme* couldn't get more *fatale* than that.

Certainly, no one would confuse these new magazines, most of them digest-size and printed on pulp paper, with the larger, slicker *Esquire*. At the same time, these new publications were taking away some of the pinup market *Esquire* had cornered during the war years. And it was a lucrative market, indeed. According to a report by the Audit Bureau of Circulation, men's magazines showed a circulation growth of 134 percent in the years between 1940 and 1949.[11] The real competitor for *Esquire*'s audience in the late 1940s, however, was not the pinup imitators but a revamped *True* magazine.

Initially, *True* was an action/adventure pulp magazine started in 1936 by Ralph Daigh, who was working for Fawcett Publications in Robbinsdale, Minnesota. Early issues of the magazine included true-life he-man hunting stories and outdoor adventures, unlike *Esquire*, which featured fiction that was not tied to a theme of violent maleness. Other features in *True* emphasized crime, sports, speed, or sex. *True* was converted into a slick magazine in 1943, with Bill Williams, the former editor of *Mechanix Illustrated*, as editor. Williams, who routinely downed a full bottle of brandy after a meal to settle his stomach, conducted most of his business from a bar. With the *Esquire* formula as a model, he began attracting famous writers to the *True* pages—Paul Gallico, Quentin Reynolds, Budd Schulberg, C. S. Forester, Robert Ruark, MacKinlay Kantor—by paying up to two thousand dollars a story. The high pay for famous bylines was not, however, a part of *Esquire*'s success. Smart and Gingrich were famous for editorial freedom but low rates for authors. By 1948, when Williams died, *True* had a circulation of more than a million. It was the first men's magazine with that many readers.[12]

Williams was succeeded as editor in 1948 by Ken W. Purdy, who increased its level of sophistication and banned fiction from its pages. "The fact is, that men don't read magazine fiction anymore. They still want good reading, good stories, but they like them better when they know they're true."[13] Years later, Tom Wolfe, the great advocate of the "New Journalism," which flourished in *Esquire* in the 1960s, would say that *True*, along with *The New Yorker*, was the spawning ground for that new literary form.[14] But adding innovative writing was not the only way *True* imitated *Esquire*. In January 1945, the Petty Girl began appearing in *True*; by 1951 portraits of starlets painted by Alberto Vargas were included in Purdy's magazine as well.

Esquire floundered in response to its competition. Its once-sophisticated writing was replaced by articles on bowling, how to add an extra closet to a bedroom, automobiles, and how to get rich quick. Add to that the *Esquire* problem with illustrations. Smart and Birmingham couldn't find a pinup artist with Vargas's popularity. In the postwar 1940s *Esquire* published girl paintings by Fritz Willis, Al Moore, Ben-Hur Boz, Ernest Chiriaka, Eddie Chan, Robert Patterson, Mauro Scali, Roswell Keller, Ward Brackette, and Ren Wicks. None of them captured the public's imagination. A readership survey published in *Esquire* in March 1948 showed that the average age of the magazine's reader was 38.7. Almost 10 percent of the readers were skilled or semiskilled laborers. Only 41 percent called themselves professionals. The survey also showed that readers had been subscribing to *Esquire* for seven or

from the days of World War II and the Varga Girl. "The Magazine
For Men" had become nostalgia at a time when Americans had more
disposable income then ever before. The change was reflected in
Esquire's advertising as well as in its editorial content. In April 1948
Hart Schaffner and Marx dropped from the magazine's pages. A year
later Kuppenheimer was gone. The back cover, reserved almost from
its beginning for top-of-the-line whiskeys like I. W. Harper, now carried ads for Pabst Blue Ribbon Beer.

To stem the tide of blue-chip advertisers who were abandoning
Esquire, David Smart tried a bizarre solution. Two brothers, G. T.
and John Sweetser, came to work as advertising salesmen at the magazine. Both were well-known amateur golfers, and Smart figured their
prowess on the links would give them entree to the better country
clubs and thus to advertisers they would win over on the nineteenth
hole. G. W. Sweetser was named publisher of *Esquire* and his brother
was made advertising director in December 1948. Smart listed himself on the *Esquire* masthead as president. The golfing gambit failed,
and a year later, in January 1950, both Sweetsers had vanished from
the magazine.[15]

The same year the Sweetser brothers left *Esquire*, a new employee
arrived in the promotion department with an assignment to write direct mail advertising for the magazine. His name was Hugh Marston
Hefner. Working for *Esquire* was a dream come true for this twenty-
four-year-old Nebraska boy. Hefner was born on April 9, 1926, in
Wahoo, Nebraska, the son of Glenn and Grace Swanson Hefner. Both
Glenn and Grace were children of Nebraska farmers. Glenn Hefner
was born in a sod hut with a dirt floor in Holdredge. He worked his
way through Nebraska Wesleyan University, graduated in 1918, and
three years later married his high school sweetheart. Both were de-
vout Methodists. When Hugh Hefner was four years old, his family
moved to Chicago and lived in a two-story brick house on the West
Side. Glenn was working as an accountant for the Advance Alu-
minium Casting Corporation.[16]

Hefner's home was an austere one; no drinking, smoking, swear-
ing, or card playing were allowed. There was an occasional Saturday
movie for Hugh and his younger brother, Keith, but Sunday was
God's day. Not even a radio could be played inside the Hefner house-
hold, and if the boys got restless they were sent outside to sit at a

backyard workbench and draw or sculpt with modeling clay. Young Hugh Hefner had an IQ of 152, but his mind wandered during class, and teachers sent notes home to Grace complaining about him. His teachers suggested his academic performance might improve if his artistic talents, which they believed to be considerable, were encouraged. Against her better judgment, Grace Hefner allowed Hugh to cover his walls with pinups from *Esquire* by George Petty and Alberto Vargas. After all, she reasoned, they *were* art.[17]

In grammar school, Hefner started a newspaper and first tried his hand as a cartoonist. Later, at Steinmetz High School, he did radio broadcasts for the Board of Education, acted in class plays, and was elected president of the student council and vice-president of the literary club. He graduated in 1944 and volunteered for the army, was discharged in 1946, and enrolled in the University of Illinois, where he dated a woman he had met in high school, Mildred Williams. Hefner sang with a local dance band, started a campus humor magazine, and saw his cartoons and articles published in the school paper. During these years on the campus at Urbana, Hefner rebelled against his parents and proclaimed himself an agnostic. He wrote a play that declared that God did not exist and this knowledge was kept from the people by the government. And he read the Kinsey report, *Sexual Behavior in the Human Male*, and *Esquire*. Hefner graduated in February 1949, married Mildred Williams, and began a life that seemed cursed by failure.

He applied for jobs on every newspaper and magazine in Chicago and was turned down by all of them; his ideas for two comic strips were rejected by all the national syndicates. He worked briefly and without pay as a movie reviewer for a Chicago entertainment magazine, but it folded after a couple of issues. He finally landed a job in the personnel department of a Chicago company that manufactured cardboard boxes, but quit in protest after a couple of months when he realized the company wouldn't hire African Americans, Jews, or anyone with a foreign-sounding name.[18] Hugh and Mildred lived off her income as a Chicago schoolteacher and moved in with Hugh's parents to cut expenses. While she worked, he stayed at home and worked on new ideas for cartoons. In 1950 he followed the course the educated unemployed have followed for years—he enrolled in graduate school. At Northwestern University he studied sociology and wrote a term paper on "Sex Behavior and the U.S. Law." He got a B+ and, after one semester, decided graduate school was not the answer. Out of school again, he grabbed a forty-dollar-a-week job as a copywriter at Carson, Pirie, Scott, a department store in Chicago's Loop.

At night, Hefner worked on a personal project, a book of cartoons called *That Toddlin' Town*. He published the book himself with one thousand dollars he raised, distributed it to bookstores, and made the publicity rounds at newspapers, radio, and television stations. While he was promoting his book, Hefner left the department store and went to work for the Leo B. Bott advertising agency. He was fired five weeks later for spending too much time promoting his book. That's when he got his sixty-dollar-a-week job with *Esquire*.[19] Hefner thought working at *Esquire* would be like living in the pages of the magazine—a life filled with sophistication and women who looked like pinups. Instead, he found it to be just another office job. A year later, in 1951, his *Esquire* job ended. David Smart decided to move the magazine to New York. Hefner was offered a cost-of-living raise and invited to come to New York, but he turned it down and stayed in Chicago.

The move to New York was urged by Abe Blinder, *Esquire*'s circulation director, and Alfred Smart, David's brother and second-in-command.[20] The advertising community in America was more and more centralized by the early 1950s—on Madison Avenue in Manhattan. Any other address, from Long Island to Los Angeles, was an outpost. And in Chicago, even though there was a top amateur golfer as publisher, *Esquire* was an outpost. Never mind that the magazine had a New York office. Both Blinder and Alfred Smart believed blue-chip advertising, which had been melting away, could be restored to the magazine if it moved to New York.

A New York location meant another change that didn't sit well with David Smart. In Chicago, the magazine was in the *Esquire* building and Smart was a celebrity. In New York, he located at 488 Madison Avenue only to find out, after he signed the lease, that the building also housed *Look* magazine and was, in fact, known as the *Look* Building. The landlord had agreed to give it that title when the weekly picture magazine moved in. Smart sued to prevent *Look*, which was published by Gardner Cowles, Jr., from claiming the edifice as its own, but was unsuccessful. So Smart and his staff settled into offices under the shadow of the giant picture magazine. *Esquire* was on the fourth floor of the building, *Look* was on the tenth, and William Weintraub, Smart's partner when *Esquire* began, had an office for his public relations firm on the seventeenth. Below Weintraub, on the fourteenth floor, was Arnold Gingrich's office. He was working as editorial director of *Flair* magazine, edited by Gardner Cowles's wife, Fleur.

After leaving *Esquire* in 1945 Gingrich had moved to Switzerland and bought a modest vineyard. Switzerland intrigued him, but working as a vintager bored him. By 1946 he was involved as editor of *Moment*, a stillborn European arts magazine. In 1949, when there was still no *Moment*, Gingrich was enticed back to the United States by Gardner Cowles, who said he was launching a liberal Republican monthly. By the time Gingrich arrived, the direction of the magazine had changed. Cowles named his wife, Fleur Fenton Cowles, as editor and *Flair* became a publication that promised to be "a magazine which combines, for the first time under one set of covers, the best in the arts: literature, fashion, humor, decoration, travel and entertainment."[21] What was most impressive about the new magazine was its physical qualities—five printing plants were used to produce each issue, which was filled with different paper stocks, insets, gatefolds, pullouts, and peepholes. The magazine lasted only a year. It had a circulation of two hundred thousand, but in its entire short life sold only 180 pages of advertising. Gingrich later called the magazine "a pansy's home journal," and said most of the editorial staff "could fly back and forth without using the stairs."[22] Once *Flair* died, Gingrich moved up four floors and went to work for Weintraub.

On February 4, 1951, Gingrich returned from a cross-country road trip with Weintraub and was in bed nursing a cold when he received a call from David Smart. The publisher's younger brother, Alfred, had died unexpectedly at age fifty-six. Alfred Smart, the heir-apparent at *Esquire*, was the opposite of his older brother. David was brash and mercurial; Alfred was calm, thoughtful, almost rabbinical.[23] David Smart smoked, drank, and took self-prescribed pills dictated by his hypochondria. Alfred never smoked, eschewed alcohol, kept in shape, took no medicine, and went on vacations with his family doctor. And now he was dead. "I have stood with a woman at the foot of a mountain precipice from whose top her husband had just fallen to his death," Gingrich wrote years later, "and twice I have been the last person to whom suicides have spoken . . . but I have never spoken to another soul as shattered as Dave was when his brother Alfred died."[24]

Without his brother, Smart seemed unable to function. From the beginning he had always had a partner—first Weintraub, then Gingrich, then Alfred. David Smart might make rash decisions, like firing seven advertising salesmen on Christmas Eve with curt notes saying, "Don't come Monday," but he always had his partners to support him. Now he was alone. He turned to Abe Blinder, his longtime circulation director, and made him executive vice-president.[25] But Blinder's expertise was in business, and *Esquire*'s editorial product was also moribund. So, in the summer of 1952, a little more than a year after Alfred Smart's death and as David Smart's misery with migraine headaches increased, *Esquire*'s publisher began courting Arnold Gingrich again.

First, Helene Richards, one of Smart's cousins who was Gingrich's old secretary, suggested he come back to *Esquire*. Then Gingrich met with Smart for coffee, but nothing about Gingrich's return was discussed. A week later, late at night, Gingrich got a phone call from Abe Blinder. Blinder said Smart wanted him to call and see if Gingrich would consider coming back to *Esquire*. Dave had changed, Blinder said, and he was more mellow and less likely to go off on tangents. Gingrich agreed to meet Smart for lunch at the Stork Club the next day. Smart told Gingrich he would no longer meddle in editorial affairs and agreed never to second-guess Gingrich again.[26] Then he popped the question. Gingrich said yes, and the odd couple were together again. This time Gingrich's title was associate publisher. His name appeared on the *Esquire* masthead with his new title in December 1952, but by that time, the magazine was in more turmoil than ever. David Smart had died in October.

Ever since Alfred's death, David Smart's hypochondria had worsened. He insisted on more and more physical checkups, and when one revealed a small polyp in his intestine, he demanded that it be removed. His doctor was against the operation because the growth was not malignant and could be monitored by regular examinations. But Smart insisted on surgery. He hired three doctors—one to perform the operation, a second to look over the shoulder of the first, and a third to watch the doctor who was watching the doctor.[27] The operation was a success, but Smart's hypochondria killed him. He had been taking so many self-prescribed drugs that his body could not respond to his postoperative antibiotics.

When Smart died, the life began to ebb from Esky. In five years he would be little more than a stylized dot above the *i* in the *Esquire* nameplate.

David Smart was never a pleasant man, and his talent seemed to be limited to hiring good people with remarkable ability. He had the American suspicion of anything but money as the measure of a man. "Money talks and bullshit walks," or, "If you're so smart why ain't you rich," might have been his watchwords. He allowed Arnold Gingrich to devise the first *Esquire* formula of girls, gags, and quality fiction, often from big-name writers. And yet, because he signed the paychecks and had the most money, he could and did alter that formula, and he changed his sophisticated monthly for the newly urbanized man into a sex magazine.

Smart longed to be a publisher whose magazines appealed to the upper classes; the original *Coronet*, the initial plans for *Ken*, and the advent of *Minotaure,* the short-lived art magazine, all showed that. But quality was always outweighed by money, and, ultimately, David Smart's publications lost the sheen of art in his pursuit of commerce. Without Smart and the changes he made, however, all the magazines might have failed. Smart, who began his career as a hustler, trusted no one but himself. He tinkered with the editorial content of the magazine and drove Gingrich away. He refused to listen to advice about the need for a new concept for *Esquire* after World War II and watched quality advertisers vanish. And he launched new business ventures such as nurseries and educational films against the judgment of his colleagues. Eventually, however, Coronet Films was a success. A swimming-instruction film featuring Matt Mann, the swimming coach at the University of Michigan, was Smart's first, followed by a film on children by Nell Dorr, a Boston photographer.

In the end, David Smart was the personification of Esky. He was a kid born in Nebraska who moved to the West Side of Chicago and, with a crease in his pants and a shine on his shoes, moved up the economic ladder, even though he was a high school dropout. He was a womanizer and a rake who learned which wines to drink, which paintings to buy, which fork to use. Because of the wealth he acquired, few people ever questioned his ideas. The early issues of *Esquire* promised readers that a few lessons in self-help could make them appealing to a duchess even though they were ignorant clods from rural America. David Smart believed that, and his life showed that it was possible. But by the time he died at age sixty, America had changed so much that there was little room for Esky anymore.

When *Esquire* began, in 1933, college education was an expensive luxury associated with the rich and well-born. By the early fifties, when David Smart died, it was available, often free through the GI Bill, to everyone. Education could come to the masses through college, and there was not as much need for the self-help *Esquire* had offered in the 1930s. *Esquire* represented the urbanization of America, but if David Smart could have looked out the window as he lay on his deathbed, he would have seen streams of automobiles leaving the city for new homes in the suburbs. *Esquire* was for the man-about-town who believed a streak of individuality would earn him the streamlined luxuries enjoyed by captains of industry. But individualism had faded into corporate conformity by the 1950s, and those streamlined luxuries were available in a new aerodynamic style of tailfins and trapezoids that made the rounded, popeyed Esky look as old-fashioned as a Hupmobile or a Wally Byam Airstream Trailer. Streamlining was a design based on the shape of a drop of water, and its commercial prototype was the dirigible; the new tailfins also had their origin in aerodynamics, but it was a World War II fighter plane, the Lockheed P-38 Lightning, that inspired the shapes that meant speed and motion to the postwar generation.[28] The world looked different from the one that spawned *Esquire*. Esky had believed in the leisurely pursuit of chorus girls in time-honored rituals of seduction; the young man of the 1950s wanted something faster than that. He wanted something that was quick—like a bunny.

After Smart's death, Gingrich was named publisher of *Esquire* by John Smart, the youngest of the three brothers, who became president of the company. Gingrich proposed that the magazine begin speaking a "new language" that would gradually transform the publication into a competitor for the readers of Time, Inc.'s, new *Sports Illustrated* or the Curtis travel monthly, *Holiday*. After a brief middle-age flirtation with the Petty Girl, who reappeared as a gate-fold in 1954, the *Esquire* foldout became a women's fashion feature that showed models in negligees that were available in department stores (which were listed on the back of the picture). It was called "*Esquire*'s Lady Fair" and was designed to help men buy clothes for their wives or sweethearts. "Lady Fair" was changed to "Great Moments in Sport" in 1954 because Gingrich wanted to distance himself from *Playboy*.[29] Then, in 1956, the gatefold disappeared altogether. Gingrich also threw out thousands of dollars' worth of detective story and western adventure manuscripts and got rid of some of the questionable advertising (B'way Joke Book, Jail-Jamas, Vibro-Matic Walkie-Talkies, Masonic Quiz Book) that had been running in the magazine's back pages. In place of the pulpish fiction that had ruled the pages of *Esquire* in its days without Gingrich, there were, once again, contributions by some of the most distinguished authors in the United States—Philip Roth, Vance Bourjaily, Anthony West, Arthur Miller, Norman Mailer, Tennessee Williams, and Arthur Schlesinger, Jr.

Like all great editors, Gingrich edited his magazine for himself, not marketing statistics. When *Esquire* began, the editor was in his twenties and had a more robust interest in sexy cartoons and pin-ups. But his love for and appreciation of art and literature survived longer than his libido, and the new language of *Esquire* reflected that. By 1957, when *Esquire* celebrated its twenty-fifth anniversary with a 318-page issue, there were only twenty cartoons and no centerfold. The only sex in the issue was four photographs of actresses shot to represent the styles of Botticelli, Gauguin, Modigliani, and an unknown seventeenth-century Italian chiaroscuro painter. Frederick Birmingham was no longer editor; he had been replaced by a quartet of Young Turks. With Gingrich's guidance, they revolutionized the magazine industry both at *Esquire* and in other publications: Clay Felker founded *New York* magazine; Ralph Ginzburg published *Eros* and went to jail on obscenity charges for it; Harold Hayes became editor of *Esquire* and midwife to the New Journalism; and Rust Hills, as *Esquire*'s fiction editor, restored the magazine's literary tone. Esky and the original formula that had made the magazine notorious were only a memory to aging veterans.

Esky may have been only a memory in the pages of *Esquire*, but halfway across the country in Chicago, where he was born, the popeyed figure was constantly on the mind of Hugh Hefner. After leaving *Esquire* when the magazine moved to New York, Hefner went to work for $80 a week as promotions manager for Publishers Development Corporation. Owned by George von Rosen, Publishers Development Corporation published trade magazines like *Shooting Goods Retailer,* but it also published *Modern Sunbathing and Hygiene* and *Sunbathing Review,* nudist magazines; *Art Photography,* a magazine that featured nude models who looked like hardened strippers; and *Modern Man,* an outdoorsy magazine that featured advice on sailing and mountain climbing along with nude and seminude pinups.[30] Hefner also talked with fellow employees about how he wanted to publish his own magazine. In 1951, just after his daughter, Christie, was born, he tried to start a Chicago magazine called *Pulse,* which was a copy of *The New Yorker,* but that failed. A year later, he left Publishers Development Corporation and became circulation director of *Children's Activities* for $120 a week. But even though he made more money at the children's magazine, and even though he gained valuable experience in direct mail campaigns and national magazine distribution, his thoughts turned again to a magazine of his own.

"I'd like to produce a magazine for the city-bred guy—breezy, sophisticated. The girlie features would guarantee the initial sale, but the magazine would have quality too," Hefner wrote in the early 1950s in his comic autobiography, a collection of cartoons that, like a diary, chronicled his life. He saw his new magazine as a combination of the editorial quality of *Life* or *Esquire,* the explicit pictures of *Modern Sunbathing,* and the sensuality of *Wink* and *Flirt.*[31] He and an old friend, Eldon Sellers, began work on the magazine and decided to call it *Stag Party.* Ironically, *Stag* had been one of the early working titles for *Esquire.*

A few days after Hefner began working on his new magazine, he found that rights for nude pinup photographs of Marilyn Monroe were for sale. He bought them for five hundred dollars and began sending out letters to magazine distributors announcing his new publication. In the letter, he made strong references to *Esquire.* "It's [*Stag Party*] being put together by a group of people from *Esquire* who stayed here in Chicago when that magazine moved east—so you can imagine how good it's going to be." Of course, it was not a group of people from *Esquire*, it was only Hefner. The letter also pushed the Marilyn Monroe pinup.[32]

Esquire may have been speaking a new language, but from a thousand miles away, Esky's voice could still be heard. It would not be heard in *Stag Party*, however. Attorneys for *Stag*, an outdoors magazine, threatened suit, and the name was changed to *Playboy*, a title Hefner liked because it conjured up images of F. Scott Fitzgerald, one of the most prominent *Esquire* contributors. *Playboy* may have been speaking in Esky's voice, but the little man had been resurrected in a different form—he was now a rabbit in a tuxedo.

It didn't take much analysis to see that the first issue of *Playboy* (December 1953) was copied from *Esquire*. *Playboy* had a page of party jokes just like the "Goldbricking With *Esquire*" feature that magazine had carried during World War II; there were sexy cartoons based on the Kinsey Report reminiscent of *Esquire*'s days before the "New Language"; there were short stories by famous authors— Ambrose Bierce and Arthur Conan Doyle (available free because they were in the public domain); there was an article about the big-band leaders, the Dorsey Brothers, that couldn't help but remind readers of the *Esquire* jazz poll; there was a page on modern desk design that brought to mind the fanciful streamline designs by Count Alexis de Sakhoffsky in the 1930s and 1940s issues of *Esquire*; there was an article on gold-digging women, the subject that had inspired hundreds of *Esquire* cartoons; and there was the "Sweetheart of the Month," Marilyn Monroe, who was the living, photographic equivalent of the Varga Girl. *Esquire*'s first pinup was a Petty illustration of a woman in the theater; the first *Playboy* pinup was a movie star. *Playboy*'s first issue sold fifty-three thousand copies. By 1959, sales were more than a million—more than *Esquire* ever sold or would sell.

Yet *Playboy* was far more than an updated *Esquire*. Its voice may have been reminiscent of Esky, but there was a big difference. *Esquire* was grounded in the Ziegfeld Follies, a burlesque show for the upper classes. *Playboy* had its cultural roots in the movies, an art form with low ticket prices and appeal to the masses. As Gay Talese wrote in his study of Hefner in *Thy Neighbor's Wife*,

> Ever since his adolescent days as an usher at the Rockne Theater in Chicago, Hefner had been enchanted

with the movies, had accepted uncritically their most im-
probable plots, had languished in their emotions and rev-
eled in their adventures; and as he stood watching in the
darkened theater, he often wished that the lights would
never turn on, that the story on the screen would continue
indefinitely and delay forever his return to the mundane,
tidy home of his German accountant father and his prim,
Swedish mother.[33]

Theater like the *Ziegfeld Follies* offers an evening of suspended
disbelief. The movies, on the other hand, offer a new reality. As
André Bazin points out, the audience at the theater knows that the
actors and scenery end at the proscenium arch; but with cinema there
is a feeling that reality exists beyond the edges of the camera lens.
In the first volume of *What Is Cinema?* Bazin writes:

> A member of a film audience tends to identify himself
> with the film's hero by a psychological process, the result
> of which is to turn the audience into a "mass" and to ren-
> der emotions uniform. . . . Let us compare chorus girls on
> the stage and on the screen. On the screen they satisfy an
> unconscious sexual desire and when the hero joins them
> he satisfies the desire of the spectator in the proportion
> to which the latter was identified with the hero. On the
> stage the girls excite the onlooker as they would in real
> life. The result is there is no identification with the hero.
> He becomes instead an object of jealousy and envy.[34]

In the theatrical world of *Esquire* the chorus girls (Varga Girls and
Petty Girls) are exciting but, ultimately, unreal and unattainable.
Their reality is on the stage or on the pages of a magazine. Possess-
ing them is impossible; away from the lights or the easel, they do
not exist. They are anonymous, the creation of an artist's brush. But
the *Playboy* world is the world of cinema. The Playmates (as they
were called after the first issue) were photographs, not paintings.
These women existed in a world that went beyond the pages they were
printed on. Despite the airbrushing used to wipe away blemishes and
smooth out their form, Playmates were part of a photographic real-

ity that gave *Playboy* readers, acting as a mass and not as individuals, satisfaction far beyond what the Varga Girl ever did. And, like Hefner's reluctance to leave the theater and return to the mundane world of his parents' home, *Playboy* readers wished for a chance to stay in the fantasy world of the Playmate.

Hefner knew the world he was creating. From the beginning, he banned advertisements for hair restorers, trusses, slimming aids, self-improvement courses, acne cures, or athlete's-foot powders. Russell Miller observes,

> In the wonderful world of *Playboy*, men had hair on their chests as well as on their heads. They were the kind of men who were always offered the best table at a restaurant, who never had to hurl themselves in front of a waiter to be served. They were legendary Lotharios, could uncouple any known bra with one hand while expertly mixing a martini with the other. They never had their faces slapped.[35]

Esquire was a magazine that showed the newly urban man how to live in a world that was alien to him; *Playboy* created a different world of fantasy for the post–World War II American male. The hero of this world was Hefner himself. Some years before *Playboy* was first published, Hefner found out about the world of cinematic fantasy when he and a girlfriend starred in a pornographic film made by his friend Eldon Sellers.[36] Later, he became the hero of the cinematic world his magazine created, posing just out of focus in Playmate pictorials but carrying his trademark pipe so readers would have no doubt who he was. Because *Playboy* was cinematic and not theatrical, readers identified with him. They did not feel the jealousy they would in the pages of the more theatrical *Esquire*. On the surface, this seems like merely the difference between illustration and photography—the difference between comic books and movies. But the nature of photography offers an anchor of reality to the imagination that illustration lacks.

By 1955, Hefner made a change in the Playmate that gave her an even closer identification with the movies. During the first two years of publication, the models featured in the centerfold were mostly anonymous—women who had posed for photographers who sold the pictures to calendar companies. But in July 1955, the Playmate of the Month was a woman who worked in the *Playboy* circulation department. This was no professional model. The copy that accompanied her photograph read,

> We suppose it's natural to think of the pulchritudinous Playmates as existing in a World apart. Actually, potential Playmates are all around you: the new secretary at your office, the doe-eyed beauty who sat opposite you at lunch yesterday, the girl who sells you shirts and ties at your favorite store. We found Miss July in our own circulation department.[37]

Her name, the magazine said, was Janet Pilgrim (actually, it was Charlaine Karalus). No more anonymous girls from the chorus line like the Varga Girls. These Playmates were *real*. Of course, in another sense, they were not real at all. They were photographic stereotypes, embellished with an airbrush and existing in a contrived environment that was as much an illusion as that month's movie starlet. But, because they were seen in photographs and not paintings, one could imagine meeting Playmates, just as one could imagine going to Hollywood and meeting Marilyn Monroe. The Varga Girls were only paint. These Playmates had names and hobbies and parents and apartments—but never boyfriends. They existed, like women in films, beyond the proscenium arch where Varga Girls melted into nothing. And just as movie stars could come from humble beginnings and be transformed into royalty by Hollywood, these women were the girls next door who could become Playmates at the click of a camera. *Esquire*? It was a magazine. "The Magazine for Men," to be exact. *Playboy* was a published version of a cinematic world of fantasy. It didn't even call itself a magazine. It was "Entertainment for Men."

Even before Hugh Hefner was taping Varga Girls to his wall, David Smart had developed the bachelor style Hefner would make famous. He slept in a round bed as Hefner did later; Smart had a penthouse apartment with leather-covered walls, Hefner had the Playboy mansion; Smart escorted Ziegfeld Girls around Chicago, Hefner had his Playmates. But Smart was only a publisher who existed in reality.

He didn't insert himself in the pages of *Esquire* so directly. No one wanted to *be* David Smart. It was his magazine readers craved. Hefner, with his understanding of the psychological power of film, thrust himself into the pages of *Playboy* as the leading man, the same role he had played in the amateur pornographic film he had made a few years earlier. Smart, of course, had made films, but they were educational, grounded in reality. *Esquire* readers may have been jealous of David Smart, but they didn't want to *be* him. Hefner, on the other hand, became the printed version of a cinematic hero. Readers identified with him and cheered on his exploits just as they cheered on Humphrey Bogart or Alan Ladd.

For twenty years, *Esquire* was the symbol of male sophistication. As the times became more cinematic, as the sleek lines of streamlining were transformed into the garish trapezoids and tailfins of the consumer-rich 1950s, men wanted more than a manual to tell them how to get ahead. Sophistication, in the *Esquire* era, was acquired. In the *Playboy* years, you could have it instantly—in the pages of the magazine, at the automobile dealership, at the Playboy Club. In 1933, when Esky was born, upward mobility required work and knowledge. At the advent of the *Playboy* rabbit, all it took to be sophisticated was money, and, it seemed, everyone had enough of that. Of course, the rabbit could not have existed without Esky, who paved the way with a magazine formula, with a victory in an obscenity case, and with an emphasis on style that had never seemed masculine before.

Esquire offered only a diversion. *Playboy* was proposing a revolution. An *Esquire* reader was supposed to gain sophistication through the pages of the magazine and then, as its promotional advertising of the 1930s said, *marry* the duchess. *Playboy*, on the other hand, was promoting sophistication without marriage. First published twenty years after the seduction of that duchess, *Playboy* was urging a new morality of consumption that denied the male role as "breadwinner." In a time of suburban conformity, as the 1950s was, the message the new magazine promoted seemed subversive. According to Barbara Ehrenreich,

> Hefner himself was not a political dissident in any conventional sense, the major intellectual influence in his early life was the Kinsey Report, and he risked his own

good name only for the right to publish bare white bo-
soms. What upset him was the "conformity, togetherness,
anonymity and slow death" men were supposed to endure
when the good life, the life which he himself came to represent, was so close at hand. . . . If Hefner was a rebel, it
was only because he took the new fun morality [the 1950s
consumer ethic] seriously. As a guide to life, the new im-
perative to enjoy was in contradiction with the prescribed
discipline of "conformity" and *Playboy*'s daring lay in facing the contradiction head-on. Conformity, or "maturity,"
as it was more affirmatively labeled by the psychologists,
required unstinting effort. . . . But *Playboy* shed the bur-
densome aspects of the adult male role at a time when
businessmen were still refining the "fun morality" for
mass consumption and the gray flannel rebels were still
fumbling for responsible alternatives. . . . *Playboy* charged
into the battle of the sexes with a dollar sign on its banner. The issue was money: men made it, women wanted
it. . . . To stay free, a man had to stay single.[38]

Esquire, however, was still a magazine that promoted male conformity. Maybe it had been racy in its day, but it never advocated a
new role for men, only an enjoyment of the one prescribed by society. The old man with the showgirl at his side in the first cartoon by
George Petty was something men should aspire to be as well as a subject of satire. *Esquire*'s cartoons and short stories were about fool-
ing around, about mistresses and showgirls and willing secretaries,
but home and a wife were still considered the basis of respectable
society. David Smart *married* his Ziegfeld Girl; Hugh Hefner only
dallied with his Playmates. *Esquire* represented the good life men
could find in the leather-covered chairs in exclusive men's clubs or
college fraternity houses. *Playboy* ignored those male enclaves based
on class, status, and prestige and started its own club on a founda-
tion of new money, available sex, and bachelorhood.

When *Playboy* was first published, using the formula developed
by *Esquire*, Arnold Gingrich was fifty years old. His interests no
longer centered around Petty Girls and off-color cartoons. His tastes
were more mature. Then came *Playboy*. As he wrote in his memoirs,

Playboy was first thought of not so much as an imitation of, but rather as an extension of, one aspect of *Esquire*, and that one, the "girly" side of *Esquire*, pushed to a degree and a limit that *Esquire* itself had never even remotely approached. It was like taking a picture of somebody with a big nose, and caricaturing him to a degree that the nose became something monstrous that the relatively minute body merely followed. . . . We were speeded by *Playboy*'s swift rise to hurry the process of ridding *Esquire* of any least vestigial traces of the girly flavor that had become the dominant side of its personality with the war years. And of course, as we did so, we received a mounting volume of letters and postcards, the latter often signed with several names and saying something like "Us guys down at this filling station are going to quit you if you don't put the girls back in—and be quick about it." To those communications we would answer to the effect of "Sorry, guys, but we've gone out of the business. Still, there's a new saloon that's opened just down the street on the other side and maybe you'll be happier there."[39]

Most people today remember *Esquire* as the magazine Gingrich developed after the "girlie" days—a publication best known for its quality short stories, its nurturing of the New Journalism, its Dubious Achievement Awards, its emphasis on the intellect, its promotion of fashion. Much of that came about after the disappearance of Esky, who vanished from the cover about the same time the pinups left the centerfold. But Esky was not really gone. He just awoke one day and found himself back in Chicago, metamorphosed into a rabbit.

Afterword

Esquire continued long after Esky, but in different incarnations. The first change came under Arnold Gingrich who, after David Smart's death, was named publisher of the magazine. Despite his new title, he continued to edit the publication as well and decided it would compete not with *Playboy*, which had stolen its World War II format, but with the newly formed Luce magazine, *Sports Illustrated*, and the upscale Curtis title, *Holiday*, a lavishly illustrated travel magazine. *Holiday* started publication in 1946, just after the end of the war, with a circulation of 450,000. By the early 1960s it was selling 939,000 copies a month and bringing in revenues of more than $10 million. *Sports Illustrated* first appeared in 1954 and within six months had a circulation of more than half a million. By 1963 it sold more than a million copies a month and had revenues of almost $18 million. Obviously, if Gingrich and *Esquire* were going to abandon sex, these two magazines weren't bad examples to follow.

But *Esquire* was still a magazine for men, and that presented problems with advertisers. "I never heard much about our image in *Esquire*'s first years," Gingrich wrote in his memoirs, "but in the mid-fifties I began to be haunted by the word. You could talk yourself blue in the face to an advertising man about what the magazine was, and what it could do and what it had done, and the best you'd get would be that all that was very interesting but 'I still don't quite get your image.'. . . Just to say that we were a men's magazine was neither enough nor even very helpful. Everybody knew what a men's magazine was: *Field and Stream*—stuff like hunting and fishing. Or *Outdoor Life*. Or *Sports Afield*. Or even *Argosy* or *True*. Sure those are men's magazines. But what's *Esquire*? What's the image?"

He tried sensationalism—stories maligning various cities and states to stir up controversy—and he brought back the Petty Girl for a while. Nothing worked. Gingrich realized that for *Esquire* to succeed he would have to look for a younger audience than World

War II veterans, and to do that he would have to recruit a younger staff. After all, the editor who had been the boy wonder in the 1930s was in his fifties now and the vagaries of youth were beyond his ken. So he hired a staff half his age that he was soon to call the Young Turks: Henry Wolfe was *Esquire*'s art director, Clay Felker was feature editor, Rust Hills was fiction editor, Ralph Ginzburg was articles editor, and Harold Hayes was assistant to the publisher.

"Within the first two weeks of their arrival each of us had decided to see how quickly we could kill off the other two," Harold Hayes wrote in *The New Republic.* "Arnold presided over this grisly circus with equanimity; in the end he usually went with the one still standing."

"The whole gang . . . used to squeeze in my office on Friday afternoons," Gingrich wrote. "The legendary explanation for the choice of Fridays being that it gave us until Monday to wash down the blood on the walls. I was generally accused of running a schedule of cockfights or a battle royal under the cover of an editorial staff meeting. . . . [It was] a test of lung power, to see who could shout everyone else down."

In a short story, "The Blood of a Wig," Terry Southern provides a thinly disguised portrait of Gingrich (called old Hacker, the publisher and editor-in-chief of *Lance,* the magazine for men) and his role in these meetings:

> "Okay," said Hack, lighting a new cigar, "suppose *I* come up with an idea? I mean, I don't wantta *surprise* you guys, cause any *heart attacks* . . . by me coming up with an *idea*," he saying this with a benign serpent smile, then adding in grim significance, "*after twenty-seven years in this goddamn game!*" He took a sip of water, as though trying to cool his irritation at being (as per usual) "the only slob around here who delivers." "Now let's just stroke this one for a while," he said, "and see if it gets stiff."

The blood-on-the-wall meetings may have been rough, but they produced results. *Esquire* became the hottest magazine of the 1960s, and its literary reputation soared beyond the heights the magazine had reached in the 1930s. Much of that came after the dust settled in the race for editor, however. Harold Hayes won. "I took him in like the morning paper," Gingrich wrote about his protégé. The other two contenders for the editor's job, Ginzburg and Felker, made magazine history elsewhere. Ginzburg became editor of *Eros* and *Avant Garde*, both sophisticated sex magazines that got him in trouble with postal authorities. Felker went to work for the *New York Herald Tribune*, where he edited *New York*, the newspaper's Sunday magazine. When the paper folded, Felker made what was once a Sunday supplement into one of America's premier local magazines.

Back at *Esquire*, Hayes was publishing such authors as Norman Mailer, James Baldwin, Saul Bellow, Gore Vidal, William Styron, Tennessee Williams, William Burroughs, Malcolm Muggeridge, and Martin Mayer. As impressive as the big names are, they pale beside the major literary achievement of *Esquire* in the 1960s—the creation, or at least popularization, of a new form of writing. That, of course, is New Journalism, factual writing that reads like fiction. The form began in *Esquire* with stories by Gay Talese and became best known in the work of Tom Wolfe. It continued with reportorial pieces by Jean Genet, who covered the 1968 Democratic Convention for the magazine; John Sack, who wrote about the Vietnam war; and Norman Mailer, who covered John Kennedy's election in 1960, wrote a novel (*An American Dream*) in monthly installments, and had a regular column, "The Big Bite." Mailer was to *Esquire* in the 1960s what Hemingway had been in the 1930s—the hairy literary chest. Although Gingrich respected most of the new writers, Mailer was an exception. As Harold Hayes wrote later, "Perhaps [it was] because he had known so well the original Mailer was noisily trying to emulate."

Gingrich continued to keep a close eye on *Esquire*'s editorial content, and he and Hayes agreed that either could have veto power over an offending item in the magazine. But Gingrich never objected, even when the outrageous *Esquire* covers by George Lois (Andy Warhol falling into a can of Campbell's tomato soup, or Hubert Humphrey as a Lyndon Johnson ventriloquist dummy, for example) caused controversy on *Esquire*'s board of directors. Gingrich's genius in those days was in allowing Hayes and his staff to take the magazine in a direction that would appeal to younger readers. Fiction changed under Hayes as well. Rust Hills was replaced as fiction editor by Gordon Lish, who published more experimental writing than either Hills or Gingrich liked. In addition to its literary wares, the 1960s *Esquire* also included the Dubious Achievement Awards, created by Robert Benton and David Newman, both of whom later left *Esquire* to write the screenplay for *Bonnie and Clyde.* Benton and Newman also created other stories—a compendium of what was in and what was out, lists of various "establishments" (art, literary, journalism, film), and a list of the one hundred best people in the world as defined by the editors.

The *Esquire* attitude was described by Hayes in his introduction to *Smiling Through the Apocalypse: Esquire's History of the Sixties:*

> Few magazines have successfully defined their own attitude, and *Esquire* is no exception. For a while we called ours an effort toward a rational view, then satire, then irony. But only humor—of a most complex, unfunny sort—is sufficiently flexible to cover the larger part of our effort, from black wit to custard-pie burlesque. Against the aridity of the national landscape of the late Fifties we offered to our readers in our better moments the promise of outright laughter; by the end of the Sixties the best we could provide was a bleak grin.

In 1974, Gingrich turned seventy and was obliged by Esquire, Inc., corporate rules to give up his title as publisher. The plan was for Hayes to move into that job, and a new editor would be named. Instead, Hayes proposed that he be named both editor and publisher. The board of directors rejected the plan (only Gingrich voted for it), and Hayes left *Esquire.* Two years later, Gingrich died of lung cancer.

Gingrich's method of editing a magazine to suit himself had become impossible to continue. By the 1970s magazines were based on marketing surveys, target audiences, and demographic surveys. Literature had little to do with it. Don Erickson, who succeeded Hayes as editor, said in a tribute to his old boss: "He did what he liked and it worked. Probably that cannot happen anymore, at least not in the magazine world, at least not the way he did it, and it saddened him at the last to realize it. Because he had had such pleasure with it—all those sentences, all those pages, all those pictures, and not a hint of demographics in a carload."

After Gingrich's death and Hayes's departure, the magazine floundered, and in 1977 it started bouncing from owner to owner. John Smart, who was president of Esquire, Inc., had begun quietly shopping the magazine around a year earlier. He was willing to sell as long as the prospective buyer would not turn the magazine into some sort of sex publication. Mortimer Zuckerman, who would later buy *The Atlantic Monthly*, was approached but decided against buying a magazine that was losing both advertising and circulation. Ultimately, *Esquire* was sold to Associated News, a British corporation, which made Clay Felker the editor.

Felker had been phenomenally successful with *New York* magazine, but when the publication was sold to Rupert Murdoch, Felker left. Now he was back at *Esquire* where he had worked twenty years before. The Felker *Esquire* would not be a continuation of the Gingrich or Hayes magazine. Instead, he and magazine designer Milton Glazer changed it to a sort of quasi-newsmagazine. It looked like a clone of Felker's *New York*, which Glazer had also designed. Monthly publication was scrapped and the magazine, now called *Esquire Fortnightly*, was issued every two weeks. Instead of the New Journalism and experimental fiction, the Felker *Esquire* published a lot of stories about business and conspicuous consumption. With a new nameplate that bore no resemblance to the script that had proclaimed *Esquire* for decades, the magazine was supposed to appeal to professional men. Ultimately, it didn't appeal to anybody. By 1979, two years after he started *Esquire Fortnightly*, Felker and Associated News sold the magazine to Phillip Moffitt and Christopher Whittle.

Whittle was a magazine publisher from Knoxville, Tennessee. He and Moffitt, who were friends from college days at the University of Tennessee, formed the 13–30 Corporation in 1968. Unlike Gingrich, who disdained demographics, Whittle made his fortune with them. Targeting readers in their teens and twenties, the two men published *Nutshell, Graduate, 18 Almanac*, and *New Marriage*. When they took over *Esquire*, Whittle and Moffitt saw the project as a sort of historic restoration—preserving the magazine as it was in its early Esky days and as it became under Hayes—but with new typography and a target market of affluent, well-educated men from twenty-five to forty-five. As part of the restoration, Rust Hills, who was *Esquire* fiction editor in the 1950s, was hired back. In the first two years he owned *Esquire*, Whittle spent more than ten million dollars and never turned a profit, although the magazine began to reestablish a reputation for good writing. Eventually, *Esquire* began to make money after Whittle stabilized a circulation base of 650,000 and increased newsstand sales from 60,000 to 120,000. But the increased circulation didn't impress advertisers. Advertising sales dropped, Moffitt left, and *Esquire* was for sale again in the mid-1980s. In December 1986, the Hearst Corporation bought the magazine from Whittle.

When Hearst took over *Esquire*, the market for men's magazines was far different than when Whittle took over the publication. By the mid-1980s, there was another player—*GQ*. Ironically, *GQ* was originally an *Esquire* magazine. At first, as *Gentlemen's Quarterly*, it was one of the menswear catalogues published by David Smart in the 1930s. Later, in 1957, the title *Gentlemen's Quarterly* was given to the old *Apparel Arts* magazine that had been *Esquire*'s precursor. *Gentlemen's Quarterly* was a fashion magazine issued four times a year, as the name implied, and was filled with articles and pictures about menswear. The old *Apparel Arts* had been a trade magazine; the new *Gentleman's Quarterly* was for consumers. There was no fiction, no sex, no articles about anything but clothes. Then, in 1979, the same year Clay Felker took over *Esquire*, Condé Nast bought *Gentlemen's Quarterly* from Esquire, Inc. Until 1979, Condé Nast had no title in the men's magazine field, but with *Gentlemen's Quarterly* in its stable, the giant publishing company, owned by the Newhouse family, started to compete with *Esquire*. The title was changed to *GQ*, more general features were added to the fashion coverage, and publication was changed from quarterly to monthly. By 1986, *GQ* had become a formidable competitor.

Still, there was the problem Gingrich had faced when he desexed *Esquire* in the 1950s. What *was* a general men's magazine? Like all parts of the magazine market, men's magazines had become special interest publications. For sex, there were *Playboy*, *Penthouse*, and *Hustler*. For sports there was not only *Sports Illustrated* but specialized titles like *Sport*, *Tennis*, *Tennis World*, *Runner's World*, *Jogging and Running Times*, *Golf*, *Golf Digest*, *Golf World*, *Racquetball*

Illustrated, and *Skin Diver.* And, of course, *GQ* had fashion. *True*, along with *Saga* and *Stag*, had macho readers. What was left for *Esquire?*

Hearst devised a new *Esquire* formula that involved heavy coverage of young movie stars, fashion, and fiction. While *Esquire* tried to rebuild, even more new competition appeared. *Details*, a Condé Nast publication designed to sell fashion to young men in their twenties, hit the newsstands in 1989. Terry McDonnell, *Esquire*'s editor, coped. But nothing seemed to improve the magazine's standing. By 1993, it was falling behind *GQ* in advertising and *Details* was closing in from behind. In October 1993, just as the sixtieth anniversary issue of *Esquire* was being unveiled, McDonnell was fired and replaced with Edward Kosner, the longtime editor of *New York.* Kosner restored some of the attitude of the Hayes *Esquire*, and more important, he gave the magazine a sort of theme. The May 1994 issue promoted what some would call a feminist backlash article by Harry Stein titled "How To Be a Man."

Being a man, of course, was what *Esquire* had been about when it began, but in 1933, when the worlds of men and women were separate, it was much easier. Sixty years later, the women's movement had changed men's perception of themselves. It was not enough to dress well, know good manners, read the right books, and see the best movies. You had to avoid being a sexist. In 1976, Alan Alda was writing about sensitive men in *Ms.* and decrying the "testosterone poisoning" most males had. The original *Esquire* showed newly urbanized men how to acquire the knowledge, clothes, and manners needed to get ahead in the city. The new mission of the magazine, it seems, is to show men how to get along in a society where maleness itself often seems in question. In "How To Be a Man," Harry Stein declares independence from the sensitive man created by feminists. "Suddenly, among guys across the social spectrum, there is a growing recognition that this business of allowing women to dictate the terms in the ongoing exchange between the sexes has been a disaster. . . . After all, this new improved man [is] . . . basically a woman with a penis." Stein proposes a "post-sensitive man," whom he describes as "at once sensitive and capable of terrific insensitivity. Thoughtful and crude. Supportive and self-absorbed. And, in almost every circumstance, able somehow to think hard about two things at once. Like, say, a domestic-policy briefing and what's under the tight, pinstripe business suit of the woman delivering it."

Kosner followed the "post-sensitive man" with a blend of past and present—Norman Mailer interviewing Madonna. He also brought back Esky, although the redesigned character should more properly be called Son of Esky: his mustache has been trimmed from its walrus dimensions to post-Yuppie neatness, his hair—apparently through transplants or a rug—no longer recedes and is neatly coiffed, and his smile is much more toothy. But he still has pop eyes, although he won't be staring at paintings of Petty Girls or Varga Girls anymore. Instead, he ogles some photomechanical aberration called the "New Varga Girl." Perhaps Esky can still teach a young man how to woo and marry the duchess. Perhaps what *Esquire* needs is a touch of history to give it a distinctiveness the newer men's magazines don't have. Who knows? But after ten years of waffling circulation, an ambivalent place in the men's magazine market, and stagnant advertising lineage, Kosner's prescription for *Esquire* is like eating chicken soup for a cold.

It couldn't hurt.

Notable Writers
in *Esquire*

Historically, *Esquire*'s fiction, particularly the fiction published in the thirties, has had more lasting impact than any other feature of the magazine. Gingrich's taste for the unconventional, his ability to attract "name" writers, and his policy that he who edits least edits best made the magazine a natural home for many authors. Stories printed in that decade included:

Ernest Hemingway, "The Snows of Kilimanjaro" (August 1936), "The Butterfly and the Tank" (December 1938), "The Denunciation" (November 1938), "The Horns of the Bull" (June 1936), "Night Before Battle" (February 1939), and "The Tradesman's Return" (February 1936).

F. Scott Fitzgerald, "The Crack Up" (February 1936), "An Alcoholic Case" (February 1937), "An Author's Mother" (September 1936), "Design in Plaster" (November 1939), "The Fiend" (January 1935), "Financing Finnegan" (January 1938), "The Guest in Room Nineteen" (October 1937), "The Honor of the Goon" (June 1937), "I Didn't Get Over" (October 1936), "In the Holidays" (December 1937), "The Long Way Out" (September 1937), "The Lost Decade" (December 1939), "The Night Before Chancellorsville" (February 1935), "Send Me In, Coach" (November 1936), "Shaggy's Morning" (May 1935), "Sleeping and Waking" (December 1934), and "Three Acts of Music" (May 1936).

W. R. Burnett, "For Charity's Sake" (January 1934), and "Greyhound Racing" (February 1936).

Erskine Caldwell, "Martha Jean" (January 1935), "Candy Man" (February 1935), "Return to Lavinia" (December 1935), "The Sick Horse" (March 1934), and "The People vs. Abe Lathan, Colored" (August 1939).

Jack Conroy, "Happy Birthday to You" (January 1937).

John Dos Passos, "Art and Isadora" (March 1936), "The Big

Director" (May 1936), "The Celebrity" (August 1935), "None But the Brave" (January 1936), and "The Camera Eye" (April 1936).

Theodore Dreiser, "The Tithe of the Lord" (January 1938).

Daniel Fuchs, "Give Hollywood a Chance" (December 1938), and "The Woman in Buffalo" (April 1939).

Chester Himes, "Crazy in Stir" (August 1934), "Every Opportunity" (May 1937), "The Night For Cryin'" (January 1937), "To What Red Hell" (October 1934), and "The Visiting Hour" (September 1936).

Langston Hughes, "Air Raid: Barcelona" (October 1938), "The Folks at Home" (May 1934), "A Good Job Gone" (April 1934), "On The Road" (January 1935), "Slice 'Em Down" (May 1936), and "Tragedy at the Baths" (October 1935).

Eric Knight, "Mary Ann and the Duke" (December 1937), "Never Come Monday" (March 1938), "Strong in the Arms" (April 1938), and "Time for the Pie-Boy" (June 1938).

Horace McCoy, "Grandstand Complex" (December 1935).

John O'Hara, "Little 'Chita" (August 1936).

John Steinbeck, "The Ears of Johnny Bear" (September 1937), "A Snake of One's Own" (February 1938), and "The Lonesome Vigilante" (October 1936).

Ira Wolfert, "Off the Highway" (October 1937).

Notes

1 When a Highbrow Meets a Lowbrow

1   John Tebbel and Mary Ellen Zuckerman, *The Magazine in America, 1741–1990*. (New York: Oxford University Press, 1991), 33–36.

2   Theodore Peterson, *Magazines in the Twentieth Century* (Urbana: University of Illinois Press, 1964), 218.

3   Geoffrey T. Hellman, "That Was New York: Crowninshield," *The New Yorker*, February 14, 1948, 72.

4   Robert C. Allen, *Horrible Prettiness: Burlesque and American Culture* (Chapel Hill: The University of North Carolina Press, 1991), 26.

5   Irving Zeidman, *The American Burlesque Show* (New York: Hawthorn Books, 1967).

6   Charles Higham, *Ziegfeld* (Chicago: Regnery, 1972), 13.

7   Andrew Ross, *No Respect: Intellectuals and Popular Culture* (New York: Routledge, 1989), 177.

8   Donald J. Bush, *The Streamlined Decade* (New York: G. Braziller, 1975), 17–21.

9   Marjorie Farnsworth, *The Ziegfeld Follies* (New York: Putnam, 1965), 84.

10   Reid Austin and Alberto Vargas, *Vargas* (New York: Harmony Books, 1978), 24.

11   Arnold Gingrich, *Nothing But People* (New York: Crown, 1971), 240–241.

12   Farnsworth, *The Ziegfeld Follies*, 11.

13   Theodore Peterson, "Some Words and Pictures about Arnold Gingrich, founding editor of Esquire, 1903–1976," *Esquire*, October 1976, 70.

14   Kevin Brownlow, *Behind the Mask of Innocence: Sex, Violence, Prejudice, Crime: Films of Social Conscience in the Silent Era* (New York: Knopf, 1990), 28.

15   Lary May, *Screening Out the Past: The Birth of Mass Culture and the Motion Picture Industry* (New York: Oxford University Press, 1980), 257.

16   Henry F. Pringle, "Sex, Esq.," *Scribner's*, March 1938, 33.

17   *"Scribner's* to the Smoking Room," *Time*, September 4, 1939, 34.

18   Lawrence W. Levine, *Highbrow Lowbrow: The Emergence of Cultural Hierarchy in America* (Cambridge: Harvard University Press, 1988), 136.

19   Ibid., 210.

2 Gingrich and Smart

1   Peterson, "Some Words and Pictures about Arnold Gingrich," 70.

2   Arnold Gingrich to Dr. Russell L. Gingrich, February 1, 1963, Arnold Gingrich Papers, Michigan Historical Collections, Bentley Historical Library, University of Michigan.

3   From sheet entitled "Information for Family Record," Arnold Gingrich Papers, Michigan Historical Collections, Bentley Historical Library, University of Michigan.

4   Arnold Gingrich to R. P. Hurst, September 25, 1935, Arnold Gingrich Papers, Michigan Historical Collections, Bentley Historical Library, University of Michigan.

5   Arnold Gingrich, *Toys of a Lifetime* (New York: Knopf, 1966).

6   "Our Man at *Esquire,*" *The Grand Rapids Press*, June 29, 1975.

7   Arnold Gingrich, *Cast Down the Laurel* (New York: Knopf, 1935).

8   Willis Frederick Dunbar, *Michigan: A History of the Wolverine State* (Grand Rapids: William B. Eerdmans, 1965), 482.

9   Michigan State Administrative Board, *Michigan: A Guide to the Wolverine State* (New York: Oxford University Press, 1941), 310.

10   Gingrich, *Toys of a Lifetime*, 78.

11   Ibid., 147.

12   Ibid., 82.

13   Note attached to a souvenir doll donated by Gingrich to charity and owned by Mr. and Mrs. Frank Wright, Michigan Historical Collections, Bentley Historical Library, University of Michigan.

14   Gingrich, *Toys of a Lifetime*, 193.

15   Arnold Gingrich to Mrs. Leo Gingrich, July 14, 1965, Arnold Gingrich Papers, Michigan Historical Collections, Bentley Historical Library, University of Michigan.

16　"Our Man at *Esquire*."

17　Gingrich, *Toys of a Lifetime*, 193.

18　"Our Man at *Esquire*."

19　Ibid.

20　Gingrich, "Scott, Ernest and Whoever," *Esquire*, October 1973.

21　"Our Man at *Esquire*."

22　High school notes of Arnold Gingrich, Arnold Gingrich Papers, Michigan Historical Collections, Bentley Historical Library, University of Michigan.

23　"Our Man at *Esquire*."

24　"William S. Rowe, Leader in Many Enterprises, Dies," *Grand Rapids Herald*, May 18, 1923.

25　Peterson, *Magazines in the Twentieth Century*, 278.

26　"Our Man at *Esquire*."

27　Harold Hayes, "Arnold Gingrich: Esquire," *The New Republic*, September 4, 1976.

28　Gingrich, *Cast Down the Laurel*.

29　"Information for Family Record."

30　"Our Man at *Esquire*."

31　Arnold Gingrich biography, from a folder labeled "Early *Esquire* Library, Arnold Gingrich Papers, Michigan Historical Collections, Bentley Historical Library, University of Michigan; Gingrich, *Toys of a Lifetime*, 156; "Our Man at *Esquire*."

32　"W. S. Rowe, Head of Mill Industry, Ill Long, Is Dead," *Grand Rapids Press*, May 18, 1923; "Information for Family Record."

33　Gingrich, *Toys of a Lifetime*, 158.

34　"Information for Family Record"; Arnold Gingrich biography, from a folder labeled "Early *Esquire* Library."

35　Gingrich, *Toys of a Lifetime*, 161.

36　James Playsted Wood, *The Story of Advertising* (New York: Ronald Press, 1958), 285–288.

37　"Widow Gets Most of $175,000 Estate Left by William S. Rowe," *Grand Rapids Herald*, May 26, 1923.

38　Pringle, "Sex, Esq.," 33; Gingrich, *Nothing But People*, 178.

39　Kenneth Rexroth, *An Autobiographical Novel* (Garden City, N.Y.: Doubleday, 1964), 330–331.

40　Gingrich, *Toys of a Lifetime*, 187.

41　Gingrich, *Nothing But People*, 34.

42　Arnold Gingrich to R. Robinson Rowe, February 18, 1965, Arnold Gingrich Papers, Michigan Historical Collections, Bentley Historical Library, University of Michigan.

43   Interview with Martin Mayer, November 30, 1989; Gingrich, *Nothing But People*, 25.

44   Gingrich, *Toys of a Lifetime*, 243.

45   Lizabeth Cohen, *Making a New Deal: Industrial Workers in Chicago, 1919–1939* (Cambridge: Cambridge University Press, 1990), 30.

46   Harry A. Cobrin, *The Men's Clothing Industry: Colonial Through Modern Times* (New York: Fairchild Publications, 1970), 48–51.

47   Gingrich, *Nothing But People*, 21.

48   *Current Biography* (New York: H.W. Wilson, 1944).

49   Gingrich, *Nothing But People*, 149.

50   Undated memo by Arnold Gingrich, Arnold Gingrich Papers, Michigan Historical Collections, Bentley Historical Library, Ann Arbor, Michigan.

51   Gingrich, *Nothing But People*, 28.

52   Ibid.

53   Peterson, *Magazines in the Twentieth Century*, 274.

54   Gingrich, *Nothing But People*, 50; Pringle, "Sex, Esq."

55   Peterson, *Magazines in the Twentieth Century*, 274.

56   "After Fortune," *Time*, October 26, 1931, 38.

57   Gingrich, *Nothing But People*, 65.

58   Cobrin, *The Men's Clothing Industry*, 340.

59   Interview with Abe Blinder, February 4, 1993.

3 Men About Town

1   "*Scribner's* to the Smoking Room," 34.

2   Peterson, *Magazines in the Twentieth Century*, 266.

3   "Success Without Editorial Policy," *The Literary Digest*, February 6, 1937, 20.

4   Hart Schaffner and Marx, *Behind The Seams With Hart Schaffner and Marx* (Chicago: Hart Schaffner and Marx, 1942), 189.

5   M. M. Lebensburger, *Selling Men's Apparel Through Advertising* (New York: McGraw-Hill, 1939), 69–70.

6   John D'Emilio and Estelle B. Freedman, *Intimate Matters: A History of Sexuality in America* (New York: Harper and Row, 1988), 228.

7   Gingrich, *Nothing But People*, 81.

8   Interview with Martin Mayer, November 30, 1989.

9   Gingrich, *Nothing But People*, 90.

10   Carlos Baker, *Ernest Hemingway: A Life Story* (New York:

Scribner's, 1968), 304.

11   Gingrich, *Nothing But People*, 84.

12   Ibid.

13   Baker, *Hemingway*, 304.

14   Ibid.

15   John Dos Passos, cable to Pauline Pfeiffer Hemingway, quoted in Baker, *Hemingway*, 344.

16   Bernice Kert, *The Hemingway Women* (New York: W. W. Norton, 1983), 275, 489.

17   Peterson, *Magazines in the Twentieth Century*, 266.

18   *Esquire*, Fall 1933.

19   "Success Without Editorial Policy," 21.

20   "Fine People Make Dull Copy," *Esquire*, October 1934, 14A.

21   "Three Characters in Search of A Magazine That Is Unhampered by the Old Taboos," *Esquire*, January 1934, 15.

22   Matthew J. Bruccoli, *Some Sort of Epic Grandeur: The Life of F. Scott Fitzgerald* (New York: Harcourt Brace Jovanovich, 1981), 389.

23   Ibid., 405.

24   Sheila Graham and Gerald Frank, *Beloved Infidel: The Education of a Woman* (New York: Henry Holt, 1958), 207.

25   Interview with Jerry Jontry, December 1, 1989.

26   Seng-gye Tombs Curtis and Christopher Hunt, *The Airbrush Book: Art, History and Technique* (New York: Van Nostrand Reinhold, 1980), 9.

27   Ibid., 18.

28   Bush, *The Streamlined Decade*, 186.

29   Austin and Vargas, *Vargas*, 23.

30   Gingrich, *Nothing But People*, 92.

31   Gingrich, *The Bedside Esquire* (New York: Knopf, 1939), 3.

32   Maurice Horn, ed., *World Encyclopedia of Cartoons* (New York: Chelsea House, 1980), 154.

33   Bruce Kellner, ed., *The Harlem Renaissance: A Historical Dictionary of the Era.* (Westport, Conn.: Greenwood Press, 1984), 67.

34   Gingrich, *Nothing But People*, 95.

35   Ibid.

36   Ibid., 198.

37   Horn, ed., *World Encyclopedia of Cartoons*, 154.

38   Gingrich, *Esquire Cartoon Album* (London: William Heineman, Ltd., 1957), 5.

39   Pringle, "Sex, Esq.," 34.

40   Peterson, *Magazines in the Twentieth Century*, 266.

4 Esky: His Salad Days

1   Warren I. Susman, *Culture as History* (New York: Pantheon, 1984), 112.

2   B. C. Bean, *The Power of Personality* (Meriden, Conn., 1920).

3   Susman, *Culture as History*, 276.

4   *Esquire*, October 1934, 162A.

5   Theodore Dreiser, *An American Tragedy* (New York: Boni and Liveright, 1925), 389.

6   *Esquire*, Fall 1933, 6.

7   Bruce Henry, "Women Are Like Gongs," *Esquire*, December 1937, 73.

8   Pringle, "Sex, Esq.," 34.

9   "As for the Toes We Tread On," *Esquire*, October 1934, 11.

10   "Torch Song, Pianissimo, to the Piano Makers," *Esquire*, April 1941, 6.

11   "Success Without Editorial Policy," 20.

12   Celia Hilliard, "Success Sells: *Esquire*'s Chicago Success Story," *Chicago*, May 1980, 134.

13   Gingrich, *Nothing But People*, 235.

14   "Breeches Boys," *Time*, October 5, 1936, 52.

15   Interview with Martin Mayer, November 30, 1989.

16   Meyer Levin, *In Search* (New York: Horizon Press, 1950), 85.

17   "Coincidence: *Esquire* Prints Another Story Already Printed," *News-Week*, August 15, 1937, 30.

18   Levin, *In Search*, 76.

19   Ibid., 127.

20   Ibid., 143.

21   "Success Without Editorial Policy," 20.

22   Peter Monro Jack, "*Cast Down the Laurel* and Other Recent Works of Fiction," *New York Times Review of Books*, February 10, 1935.

23   Gingrich, *Nothing But People*, 140.

24   Transcripts of hearing, *Hannegan* v. *Esquire*, October 25–November 3, 1943, 1405.

25   Pringle, "Sex, Esq.," 39.

26   Esquire promotional booklet, 1936.

27   Pringle, "Sex, Esq.," 88.

28   Interview with Abe Blinder, former circulation director of *Esquire*, February 4, 1993.

29   "Saga of Smart," *Time*, May 12, 1941, 63.

30   Gingrich, *Nothing But People*, 141.

31   *"Scribner's* to the Smoking Room."

32   Peterson, *Magazines in the Twentieth Century*, 99.

33   Interview with Jerry Jontry, former advertising director of *Esquire*, December 1, 1989.

5 Other Parts of the Empire

1   "Saga of Smart," 63.

2   Henry Ringling North and Alden Hatch, *The Circus Kings* (Garden City, N.Y.: Doubleday, 1960), 178.

3   Gingrich, *Nothing But People*, 15.

4   Eric Barnouw, *The Sponsor: Notes on a Modern Potentate* (New York: Oxford University Press, 1978), 35–39.

5   Peterson, *Magazines in the Twentieth Century*, 342.

6   Interview with Oscar Dystel, August 13, 1993.

7   Tebbel and Zuckerman, *The Magazine in America*, 155.

8   Gingrich, *Nothing But People*, 153.

9   Interview with Oscar Dystel, August 13, 1993.

10   Roland E. Wolseley, *The Changing Magazine: Trends in Readership and Management* (New York: Hastings House, 1973), 46.

11   Peterson, *Magazines in the Twentieth Century*, 342.

12   "Saga of Smart," 63.

13   Interview with Oscar Dystel, August 13, 1993.

14   Wolseley, *The Changing Magazine*, 47.

15   Arnold Gingrich, address to the Association for Education in Journalism, Lincoln, Nebraska, August 28, 1963.

16   Gingrich, *Nothing But People*, 127.

17   Malcolm Haslam, *The Real World of the Surrealists* (New York: Rizzoli, 1978), 229–230.

18   Maurice Nadeau, *The History of Surrealism* (Cambridge, Mass.: Harvard University Press, 1989), 200.

19   Gingrich, *Nothing But People*, 312.

20   "Saga of Smart," 63.

21   Levin, *In Search*, 109.

22   George Seldes, *"Ken*—The Insider's Story," *The Nation*, April 30, 1938.

23   Gingrich, *Nothing But People*, 132.

24   Frank Luther Mott, *A History of American Magazines, 1865–1885* (Cambridge, Mass.: Harvard University Press, 1938).

25   Theodore H. White, *In Search of History* (New York: Atheneum, 1978).

26   David W. Levy, *Herbert Croly of* The New Republic (Princeton: Princeton University Press, 1985).

27   Leslie Fishbein, *Rebels in Bohemia: The Radicals of "The Masses"* (Chapel Hill: University of North Carolina Press, 1982).

28   White, *In Search of History*, 147.

29   Roy Hoopes, *Ralph Ingersoll, A Biography.* (New York: Atheneum, 1985).

30   Peterson, *Magazines in the Twentieth Century*, 13.

31   W. A. Swanberg, *Luce and His Empire* (New York: Scribner's, 1972).

32   Peterson, *Magazines in the Twentieth Century*, 38.

33   Seldes, "Ken," 498.

34   Baker, *Hemingway*, 403.

35   Seldes, "Ken," 497.

36   Levin, *In Search*, 110–111.

37   Interview with Oscar Dystel, August 13, 1993.

38   Gingrich, *Nothing But People*, 136.

39   Seldes, "Ken," 497.

40   Levin, *In Search*, 110.

41   Seldes, "Ken," 498.

42   Ibid.

43   Gingrich, *Nothing But People*, 138.

44   Seldes, "Ken," 498.

45   Levin, *In Search*, 128.

46   Seldes, "Ken," 499.

47   Ibid.

48   "Within the Editorial Ken," *Ken*, August 25, 1938, 4.

49   Seldes, "Ken," 499.

50   Baker, *Hemingway*, 412.

51   Editorial, *Ken*, September 8, 1938, 4.

52   Peterson, *Magazines in the Twentieth Century*, 280.

53   Tebbel and Zuckerman, *The Magazine in America*, 188.

54   Levin, *In Search*, 127–128.

55   Peterson, *Magazines in the Twentieth Century*, 280.

56   Gingrich, *Nothing But People*, 146.

6 Vargas, World War II, and All That Jazz

1   Interview with Oscar Dystel, August 23, 1993.

2   Astrid Rossana Conte, *Vargas* (Berlin: Benedikt Taschen, 1990), 8.

3   Austin and Vargas, *Vargas*, 11.

4   Ibid., 12.

5   Ibid., 22.

6   Ibid., 28.

7   Gingrich, *Nothing But People*, 196.

8   Austin and Vargas, *Vargas*, 24.

9   Kurt Vonnegut, introduction to Reid Austin, *Varga: The Esquire Years* (New York: Alfred Van Der Marck Editions, 1987), 7.

10   Interview with Jeanne Dean, February 3, 1993.

11   Austin and Vargas, *Vargas*, 32.

12   Ibid., 31.

13   Lois W. Banner, *American Beauty* (Chicago: University of Chicago Press, 1983), 283.

14   Geoff Weedon and Richard Ward, *Fairground Art: The Art Forms of Traveling Fairs, Carousels and Carnival Midways* (New York: Abbeville Press, 1981), 270.

15   "Talk of the Town," *The New Yorker*, January 11, 1941, 17.

16   John Morton Blum, *V Was for Victory: Politics and American Culture During World War II* (New York: Harcourt Brace Jovanovich, 1976), 107–108.

17   Interview with Abe Blinder, February 4, 1993.

18   Gingrich, *Nothing But People*, 158.

19   Transcript of *Hannegan* v. *Esquire*, 1392–1405.

20   Ibid.

21   Blum, *V Was For Victory*, 18.

22   "Hedda Hopper's Hollywood," July 1944. Distributed by Twentieth Century–Fox.

23   Vonnegut, in Austin, *Varga*, 6.

24   Blum, *V Was for Victory*, 70.

25   For a catalogue showing Varga Girls painted on ships and military vehicles, see Ian Logan and Henry Nield, *Classy Chassy: American Aircraft "Girl Art," 1942–1953* (New York: A. and W. Visual Library, 1977).

26   Blum, *V Was for Victory*, 37.

27   O. E. Schoeffler and William Gale, *Esquire's Encyclopedia of Twentieth Century Men's Fashions* (New York: McGraw-Hill, 1973), 26.

28   Gingrich, *Nothing But People*, 290.

29   Leonard Feather, *The Jazz Years: Earwitness to an Era* (New York: DeCapo Press, 1987), 76.

30   Ibid., 79.

31   Ibid., 80.

7 Esky Goes to Court

1   Gingrich, *Nothing But People*, 121.

2   Interview with Reid Austin, January 15, 1993.

3   Hilliard, "Sophistication Sells," 134.

4   Interview with Abe Blinder.

5   Gingrich, *Nothing But People*, 158.

6   "The Experts Failed to Blush," *Time*, November 1, 1943, 42.

7   *Current Biography* (New York: H. W. Wilson, 1940), 833–835.

8   Ted Morgan, *FDR: A Biography* (New York: Simon and Schuster, 1985), 609.

9   "*Esquire* Banned," *Time*, January 10, 1944, 46.

10   James C. Paul and Murray L. Schwartz, *Federal Censorship: Obscenity in the Mail* (New York: Free Press of Glencoe, 1961), 73.

11   Gingrich, *Nothing But People*, 159.

12   Paul and Schwartz, *Federal Censorship*, 19–23.

13   Frank Luther Mott, *A History of American Magazines, 1865–1885* (Cambridge, Mass.: Harvard University Press, 1938), 5.

14   Paul and Schwartz, *Federal Censorship*, 44–48.

15   Ibid., 64.

16   Ibid., 73.

17   Gingrich, *Nothing But People*, 159.

18   "The Experts Failed to Blush," 42.

19   39 U.S. Code, Section 226.

20   Transcript of *Hannegan* v. *Esquire*, 32–40.

21   Ibid., 1137–1155.

22   Ibid., 1576–1587.

23   Gingrich, *Nothing But People*, 163–164.

24   "The Experts Failed to Blush," 42–43.

25   Austin and Vargas, *Vargas*, 32.

26   Transcript of *Hannegan* v. *Esquire*, 1777–1778.

27   Ibid., 1812–1814.

28   Order of the Postmaster General Revoking Second Class Privileges, December 30, 1943, order number 23459, paragraphs 5586–5592.

29   "*Esquire* Banned," 46.

30   "T. Whitfield Davidson Dead, Senior Federal Judge Was 97," *The New York Times*, January 27, 1973.

31   "That Wasn't No Lady," *Newsweek* July 30, 1944, 84–86.

32   U.S. Supreme Court brief, October term 1945, no. 399, p. 6.

33   "That Wasn't No Lady," 86.

34   Gingrich, *Nothing But People*, 164.

35   Paul and Schwartz, *Federal Censorship*, 76.

36   Harry S. Truman, *Year of Decisions* (Garden City, N.Y.: Doubleday and Company, 1955), 160–161, 324.

37   Supreme Court of the United States, October term 1945, no. 399, pp. 6–9.

38   H. L. Mencken, "Editorial," *The American Mercury*, December 1928, 407–410.

39   Esquire Promotional Booklet, 1936.

40   Lary May, *Screening Out the Past: The Birth of Mass Culture and the Motion Picture Industry* (New York: Oxford University Press, 1980), 255; Motion Picture Production Code, in Murray Schumach, *The Face on the Cutting Room Floor* (New York: William Morrow, 1964), 278–292.

41   Gingrich, *Nothing But People*, 165.

42   Interview with Oscar Dystel, August 13, 1993.

43   Interview with Abe Blinder.

44   Interview with Oscar Dystel, August 13, 1993.

45   Austin and Vargas, *Vargas*, 38.

46   Ibid., 42.

47   Feather, *The Jazz Years*, 90.

48   Quoted in Feather, *The Jazz Years*, 90.

49   Armstrong et al. to David Smart, February 14, 1947, now in the collection of Leonard Feather.

50   Feather, *The Jazz Years*, 94.

8 Esky's Metamorphosis

1   Blum, *V Was For Victory*, 104.

2   Elaine Tyler May, *Homeward Bound: American Families in the Cold War Era* (New York: Basic Books, 1988), 184.

3   Interview with Frances Birmingham, widow of Frederick Birmingham, August 24, 1993.

4   Ibid.

5   Gingrich, *Nothing But People*, 167.

6   Interview with Abe Blinder.

7   Interview with Oscar Dystel, August 13, 1993.

8   Interview with Martin Meyer, November 21, 1989.

9   Interview with Abe Blinder.

10   Peterson, *Magazines in the Twentieth Century*, 378.

11   Carl Hodge, "For Men Only," *Magazine Industry*, Winter 1950, 13.

12   Peterson, *Magazines in the Twentieth Century*, 311–314.

13   Quoted in *Tide*, March 28, 1956, 56.

14   Tom Wolfe, *The New Journalism* (New York: Harper and Row, 1973), 46.

15   Interview with Oscar Dystel, October 13, 1993.

16   Russell Miller, *Bunny: The Real Story of Playboy* (New York: Holt, Rinehart and Winston, 1984), 18.

17   Gay Talese, *Thy Neighbor's Wife* (Garden City, N.Y.: Doubleday, 1980), 32.

18   Miller, *Bunny*, 25.

19   Ibid., 27.

20   Interview with Abe Blinder.

21   Peterson, *Magazines in the Twentieth Century*, 282.

22   Gingrich, *Nothing But People*, 180.

23   Interview with Oscar Dystel, August 13, 1993.

24   Gingrich, *Nothing But People*, 172.

25   Interview with Abe Blinder.

26   Gingrich, *Nothing But People*, 188.

27   Interview with Oscar Dystel, August 13, 1993.

28   Thomas Hine, *Populuxe* (New York: Alfred A. Knopf, 1986), 84.

29   Gingrich, *Nothing But People*, 194.

30   Talese, *Thy Neighbor's Wife*, 50.

31   Miller, *Bunny*, 31.

32   Ibid., 33.

33   Talese, *Thy Neighbor's Wife*, 449.

34   André Bazin, *What Is Cinema?* (Berkeley, Calif.: University of California Press, 1967), 99.

35   Miller, *Bunny*, 47.

36   Talese, *Thy Neighbor's Wife*, 50.

37   "Miss July," *Playboy*, July 1955, 64.

38   Barbara Ehrenreich, *The Hearts of Men: American Dreams and the Flight from Commitment* (New York: Anchor Press/Doubleday, 1983), 44–46.

39   Gingrich, *Nothing But People*, 95–96.

Bibliography

Interviews (all with author)

Austin, Reid. Author of unpublished biography of George Petty. January 6, 1993, Santa Fe, N.M. Telephone interview.

Birmingham, Frances. Widow of Fredrick Birmingham, former editor of *Esquire*. August 24, 1993, Scranton, Pa. Telephone interview.

Blinder, Abe. Former president of Esquire, Inc., and circulation director for *Esquire* in the 1930s and 1940s. February 4, 1993, Red Bank, N.J. Telephone interview.

Dean, Jeanne. Model for Antonio Vargas. February 3, 1993, Malibu, Calif. Telephone interview.

Dystel, Oscar. Former editor of *Coronet*. August 13, 1993, and October 13, 1993, White Plains, N.Y. Telephone interviews.

Jontry, Jerry. Former advertising director for *Esquire*. December 1, 1989, New York City. Telephone interview.

Mayer, Martin. Former copyeditor for *Esquire*. November 30, 1989, New York City. Telephone interview.

Manuscript Collections

Esquire Magazine Collection. Michigan Historical Collections, Bentley Historical Library, University of Michigan, Ann Arbor, Michigan.

Arnold Gingrich. Papers, 1932–1975. Michigan Historical Collections, Bentley Historical Library, University of Michigan, Ann Arbor, Michigan.

Federal Documents

Supreme Court of the United States, No. 399, October term, 1945. Robert E. Hannegan, as Postmaster General of the United States, Petitioner,

v. *Esquire*, Inc. February 1, 1946. Opinion by Justice Felix Frankfurter.

Supreme Court of the United States, No. 399, October term, 1945. Brief for the Postmaster General, J. Howard McGrath, Solicitor General; John F. Sonnett, Assistant Attorney General; Marvin C. Taylor, attorney; Vincent M. Miles, Solicitor, Post Office Department.

Supreme Court of the United States, No. 399, October term, 1945. Brief for *Esquire*, Bruce Bromley, Hugh Lynch, Jr.

Transcript of hearings on *Hannegan* v. *Esquire*, October 25–November 3, 1943.

Books

Allen, Robert C. *Horrible Prettiness: Burlesque and American Culture.* Chapel Hill: The University of North Carolina Press, 1991.

Austin, Reid, and Alberto Vargas. *Vargas.* New York: Harmony Books, 1978.

Baker, Carlos. *Ernest Hemingway: A Life Story.* New York: Scribner's, 1968.

Banner, Lois W. *American Beauty.* Chicago: University of Chicago Press, 1983.

Barnouw, Eric. *The Sponsor: Notes on a Modern Potentate.* New York: Oxford University Press, 1978.

Baron, Herman. *Author Index to Esquire.* Metuchen, N.J.: Scarecrow Press, 1976.

Bean, B. C. *Power of Personality.* Meriden, Conn.: Pelton Publishing, 1920.

Blum, John Morton. *V Was For Victory: Politics and American Culture During World War II.* New York: Harcourt Brace Jovanovich, 1976.

Brownlow, Kevin. *Behind the Mask of Innocence: Sex, Violence, Prejudice, Crime: Films of Social Conscience in the Silent Era.* New York: Knopf, 1990.

Bruccoli, Matthew J. *Some Sort of Epic Grandeur: The Life of F. Scott Fitzgerald.* New York: Harcourt Brace Jovanovich, 1981.

Bush, Donald J. *The Streamlined Decade.* New York: G. Braziller, 1975.

Cobrin, Harry A. *The Men's Clothing Industry: Colonial Through Modern Times.* New York: Fairchild Publications, 1970.

Cohen, Lizabeth. *Making a New Deal: Industrial Workers in Chicago, 1919–1939.* Cambridge: Cambridge University Press, 1990.

Collier, James Lincoln. *The Making of Jazz: A Comprehensive History.* New York: Houghton Mifflin, 1978.

Conte, Astrid Rossana. *Vargas.* Berlin: Benedikt Taschen, 1990.

Covert, Catherine L., and John D. Stevens, eds. *Mass Media Between the Wars: Perceptions of Cultural Tensions, 1918–1941*. Syracuse, N.Y.: Syracuse University Press, 1984.

Cronon, William. *Nature's Metropolis: Chicago and the Great West*. New York: W. W. Norton, 1991.

Curtis, Seng-gye Tombs, and Christopher Hunt. *The Airbrush Book: Art, History and Technique*. New York: Van Nostrand Reinhold, 1980.

D'Emilio, John, and Estelle B. Freedman. *Intimate Matters: A History of Sexuality in America*. New York: Harper and Row, 1988.

Draper, Robert. *Rolling Stone Magazine: The Uncensored History*. New York: Doubleday, 1990.

Dreiser, Theodore. *An American Tragedy*. New York: Boni and Liveright, 1925.

Ehrenreich, Barbara. *The Hearts of Men: American Dreams and the Flight from Commitment*. Garden City, N.Y.: Anchor Press/Doubleday, 1983.

Ewen, Stuart, and Elizabeth Ewen. *Channels of Desire: Mass Images and the Shaping of American Consciousness*. Minneapolis: University of Minnesota Press, 1982.

Farnsworth, Marjorie. *The Ziegfeld Follies*. New York: Putnam, 1965.

Feather, Leonard. *The Jazz Years: Earwitness to an Era*. New York: Da Capo Press, 1987.

Fecher, Charles A., ed. *The Diary of H. L. Mencken*. New York: Knopf, 1989.

Fishbein, Leslie. *Rebels in Bohemia: The Radicals of "The Masses."* Chapel Hill: University of North Carolina Press, 1982.

Gabor, Mark. *The Pin-Up: A Modest History*. New York: Universe Books, 1972.

Gillespie, Dizzy. *To Be or Not to Bop*. Garden City, N.Y.: Doubleday, 1979.

Gingrich, Arnold. *Cast Down the Laurel*. New York: Knopf, 1935.

———. *Esquire Cartoon Album*. New York: Knopf, 1957.

———. *Toys of a Lifetime*. New York: Knopf, 1966.

———. *Nothing But People*. New York: Crown, 1971.

Gitler, Ira. *Jazz Masters of the 40s*, New York: Macmillan, 1966.

Goldstein, Malcolm. *The Political Stage: American Drama and Theater of the Great Depression*. New York: Oxford University Press, 1974.

Graham, Sheilah, and Gerald Frank. *Beloved Infidel: The Education of a Woman*. New York: Henry Holt, 1958.

Hamalian, Linda. *A Life of Kenneth Rexroth*. New York: W. W. Norton, 1991.

Hart Schaffner and Marx. *Behind the Seams with Hart Schaffner and Marx*. Chicago: Hart Schaffner and Marx, 1942.

Haslam, Malcolm. *The Real World of the Surrealists*. New York: Rizzoli, 1978.

Higham, Charles. *Ziegfeld*. Chicago: Regnery, 1972.

Himes, Chester. *The Quality of Hurt*. London: Joseph, 1972.

Hine, Thomas. *Populuxe*. New York: Knopf, 1986.

Hoopes, Roy. *Ralph Ingersoll, A Biography*. New York: Atheneum, 1985.

Kellner, Bruce, ed. *The Harlem Renaissance: A Historical Dictionary of the Era*. Westport, Conn.: Greenwood Press, 1984.

Kert, Bernice. *The Hemingway Women*. New York: W. W. Norton, 1983.

Lebensburger, M. M. *Selling Men's Apparel through Advertising*. New York: McGraw-Hill, 1939.

Levin, Meyer. *In Search*. New York: Horizon Press, 1950.

Levine, Lawrence W. *Highbrow Lowbrow: The Emergence of Cultural Hierarchy in America*. Cambridge, Mass.: Harvard University Press, 1988.

Levy, David W. *Herbert Croly of The New Republic*. Princeton: Princeton University Press, 1985.

Logan, Ian, and Henry Nield. *Classy Chassy: American Aircraft "Girl Art," 1942–1953*. New York: A & W Visual Library, 1977.

McElvaine, Robert S. *The Great Depression: America 1929–1941*. New York: Times Books, 1984.

Madden, David, ed. *Proletarian Writers of the Thirties*. Carbondale, Ill.: University of Southern Illinois Press, 1968.

May, Elaine Tyler. *Homeward Bound: American Families in the Cold War Era*. New York: Basic Books, 1988.

May, Lary. *Screening Out the Past: The Birth of Mass Culture and the Motion Picture Industry*. New York: Oxford University Press, 1980.

Miller, Russell. *Bunny: The Real Story of Playboy*. New York: Holt, Rinehart and Winston, 1984.

Morgan, Ted. *FDR: A Biography*. New York: Simon and Schuster, 1985.

Mott, Frank Luther. *A History of American Magazines, 1865–1885*. Cambridge, Mass.: Harvard University Press, 1938.

Nadeau, Maurice. *The History of Surrealism*. Cambridge, Mass.: Harvard University Press, 1989.

Norris, James D. *Advertising and the Transformation of American Society, 1865–1920*. New York: Greenwood Press, 1990.

North, Henry Ringling, and Alden Hatch. *The Circus Kings*. Garden City, N.Y.: Doubleday, 1960.

Paul, James C., and Murray L. Schwartz. *Federal Censorship: Obscenity in the Mail*. New York: Free Press of Glencoe, 1961.

Peiss, Kathy. *Cheap Amusements: Working Women and Leisure in Turn-of-the-Century New York*. Philadelphia: Temple University Press, 1986.

Peterson, Theodore. *Magazines in the Twentieth Century*. Urbana: University of Illinois Press, 1964.

Prager, Arthur. *The Mahogany Tree: An Informal History of Punch*. New York: Hawthorne Books, 1979.

Rampersad, Arnold. *The Life of Langston Hughes, Volume 1: 1902–1941*. New York: Oxford University Press, 1986.

Rexroth, Kenneth. *An Autobiographical Novel*. Garden City, N.Y.: Doubleday, 1964.

Ross, Andrew. *No Respect: Intellectuals and Popular Culture*. New York: Routledge, 1989.

Schickel, Richard. *The Disney Version: The Life, Times, Art and Commerce of Walt Disney*. New York: Simon and Schuster, 1968.

Schoeffler, O. E., and William Gale. *Esquire's Encyclopedia of 20th Century Men's Fashions*. New York: McGraw-Hill, 1973.

Seltzer, George. *Music Matters: The Performer and the American Federation of Musicians*. Metuchen, N.J.: Scarecrow Press, 1989.

Shapiro, Nat, and Nat Hentoff. *Here Me Talkin to Ya: The Story of Jazz as Told by the Men Who Made It*. New York: Dover Publications, 1955.

Smith, Alson J. *Chicago's Left Bank*. Chicago: Regnery, 1953.

Steinberg, Salme Harju. *Reformer in the Marketplace: Edward W. Bok and The Ladies' Home Journal*. Baton Rouge: Louisiana State University Press, 1979.

Strasser, Susan. *Satisfaction Guaranteed: The Making of the American Mass Market*. New York: Pantheon, 1989.

Susman, Warren I. *Culture as History*. New York: Pantheon, 1984.

Swanberg, W. A. *Luce and His Empire*. New York: Scribner's, 1972.

Talese, Gay. *Thy Neighbor's Wife*. Garden City, N.Y.: Doubleday, 1980.

Tebbel, John, and Mary Ellen Zuckerman. *The Magazine in America, 1741–1990*. New York: Oxford University Press, 1991.

Truman, Harry S. *Year of Decisions*. Garden City, N.Y.: Doubleday, 1955.

Vargas, Alberto. *The Esquire Years*. New York: Alfred Van Der Marck Editions, 1987.

Weedon, Geoff, and Richard Ward. *Fairground Art: The Art Forms of Travelling Fairs, Carousels and Carnival Midways*. New York: Abbeville Press, 1981.

Weinhardt, Carl J. *The Most of John Held Jr.* Brattleboro, Vt.: The Stephen Greene Press, 1972.

White, Theodore. *In Search of History.* New York: Atheneum, 1978.

Wolseley, Roland E. *The Changing Magazine: Trends in Readership and Management.* New York: Hastings House, 1973.

Wood, James Playsted. *The Story of Advertising.* New York: Roland Press, 1958.

Zeidman, Irving. *The American Burlesque Show.* New York: Hawthorn Books, 1967.

Articles

"Book-Sized Magazines for Non-*Esquire* Minds." *Newsweek*, October 31, 1936, 3.

"Breeches Boys." *Time*, October 5, 1936, 52.

Cohen, Gordon L. "Esquire-Coronet's *Ken:* Magazine Everyone Hated." *Media History Digest*, Spring-Summer, 1987.

"Cowles Empire." *Business Week*, October 9, 1949, 26.

"Culture in Capsule Form." *The Literary Digest*, October 31, 1936, 43.

"Dangerous Thoughts." *The Nation*, April 22, 1950, 336.

"David Smart." *Newsweek*, October 27, 1952, 81.

"David Smart." *Time*, October 27, 1952, 103.

"Decision in U.S. Post Office v. *Esquire* Case." *Saturday Review of Literature*, June 16, 1945, 16.

"Dinna Ken." *Saturday Review of Literature*, April 9, 1938, 8.

"*Esquire* Affair." *American Mercury*, March, 1944, 317–318.

"*Esquire* Banned." *Time*, January 10, 1944, 46.

"*Esquire* Case to be Heard by Supreme Court." *Publishers Weekly*, October 27, 1945, 19.

"*Esquire* Decision." *The Reader's Digest*, October, 1944, 64.

"*Esquire* Loses." *Publishers Weekly*, July 22, 1944, 249.

"*Esquire* Loses a Round." *Business Week*, January 8, 1944, 87.

"*Esquire* Mailing Privileges Upheld." *Publishers Weekly*, February 9, 1946, 26.

"*Esquire* Wins." *Business Week*, June 9, 1945, 102.

"*Esquire* Wins Back 2nd Class Mailing." *Publishers Weekly*, June 9, 1945, 83.

"*Esquire*'s Kid Brother." *Newsweek*, April 4, 1938, 12.

"The Experts Failed to Blush." *Time*, November 1, 1943, 42.

"*Flair*'s Finish." *Newsweek*, December 11, 1950, 57.

"Fleur's *Flair.*" *Newsweek*, September 12, 1949, 57.

"Fleur's *Flair.*" *Time*, September 12, 1949, 63.

Gingrich, Arnold, "Scott, Ernest and Whoever." *Esquire*, October 1973.

"Girl with Roses." *Time*, January 30, 1950, 57.

Hayes, Harold. "Arnold Gingrich: Esquire." *The New Republic*, September 4, 1976.

Hellman, Geoffrey. "This Was New York: Crowninshield." *The New Yorker*, February 14, 1948.

Hilliard, Celia. "Sophistication Sells: *Esquire*'s Chicago Success Story." *Chicago*, May 1980.

"*Ken*'s Demise." *Newsweek*, July 10, 1939, 37.

"*Ken*'s End." *Time*, July 10, 1939, 33.

"Literary by Degrees." *Wilson Library Bulletin*, February 1944, 420.

"No Flair." *Time*, December 11, 1950, 57.

"Open Door to *Esquire.*" *Writer*, February 1949, 42.

"Our Man at *Esquire.*" *The Grand Rapids Press*, June 29, 1975.

Peterson, Theodore. "Some Words and Pictures about Arnold Gingrich, founding editor of *Esquire*, 1903–1976." *Esquire*, October 1976.

"Postmaster General Penalizes *Esquire.*" *Christian Century*, January 12, 1944, 37.

Pringle, Henry F. "Sex, Esq." *Scribner's Magazine*, March 1938.

Rao, S. Sreenvias. "Why Coronet Failed." *Journalism Quarterly*, Spring 1965, 271.

"Relief for Esky." *Newsweek*, June 11, 1945, 96.

"Saga of Smart." *Time*, May 12, 1941, 63.

"*Scribner's* to the Smoking Room." *Time*, September 4, 1939, 34.

"SEC and *Esquire.*" *Business Week*, May 17, 1941, 67.

Seldes, George. "*Ken*—The Insider's Story." *The Nation*, April 30, 1938.

"Speechless *Esquire.*" *Newsweek*, January 10, 1944, 71.

"Success Without Editorial Policy." *The Literary Digest*, February 6, 1937, 20.

"Sugar and Spice." *Newsweek*, January 30, 1950, 46.

"T. Whitfield Davidson Dead, Senior Federal Judge Was 97." *The New York Times*, January 27, 1973.

"That Wasn't No Lady." *Newsweek*, July 30, 1944, 84–86.

"Three-Way *Ken.*" *Business Week*, April 3, 1938, 36.

"Too Many Magazines." *Time*, June 17, 1946.

"Trade Winds." *Saturday Review of Literature*, February 5, 1944, 20.

"Tyranny and *Esquire.*" *Collier's*, September 16, 1944, 82.

"Widow Gets Most of $175,000 Estate Left by William S. Rowe." *Grand Rapids Herald*, May 26, 1923, 1.

"William S. Rowe, Leader in Many Enterprises, Dies." *Grand Rapids Herald*, May 18, 1923, 1.

"Within the Editorial Ken." *Ken*, August 25, 1938, 4.

"W. S. Rowe, Head of Mill Industry, Ill Long, Is Dead." *Grand Rapids Press*, May 18, 1923, 1.

Index

About the Author

Hugh Merrill is the author of *The Blues Route*, published in 1990. He has worked for more than twenty-five years as a writer and editor for magazines and newspapers throughout the South. As a writer he has worked for *The Daily News* in Atlanta, *Atlanta Weekly* magazine, *The Atlanta Journal*, *The Birmingham News*, and *The Huntsville Times*. He was editor of *The Harpeth Herald* in Nashville and *Louisville Today* magazine. In 1988 he won the National Newspaper Association award for the best column of the year. Merrill has also worked as a playwright, screenwriter, actor, magician, country music disc jockey, and political flack. He has written for *In These Times, New Observations, Atlanta Magazine, Rolling Stone, The New York Times, The Baltimore Sun,* and the Sunday magazines of *The Chicago Tribune, The Denver Post,* and *The Dallas Morning News*. Merrill has a Ph.D. in American Studies from Emory University and is currently an assistant professor of journalism at the University of West Florida. He lives in Pensacola with his wife, Jacinta, and their dog, Blue.